Table of Contents

Catholicism's Olive Branch

Reaching Out in a Fragmented Faith World

by

Dr. ant

Copyright 2024 Dr. ant. All rights reserved.

No part of this book may be reproduced in any form or by any electronic or mechanical means including information storage and retrieval systems, without permission in writing from the author. The only exception is by a reviewer, who may quote short excerpts in a review.

Although the author and publisher have made every effort to ensure that the information in this book was correct at press time, the author and publisher do not assume and hereby disclaim any liability to any party for any loss, damage, or disruption caused by errors or omissions, whether such errors or omissions result from negligence, accident, or any other cause.

This publication is designed to provide accurate and authoritative information with regard to the subject matter covered. It is sold with the understanding that the publisher is not engaged in rendering professional services. If legal advice or other expert assistance is required, the services of a competent professional should be sought.

The fact that an organization or website is referred to in this work as a citation and/or a potential source of further information does not mean that the author or the publisher endorses the information the organization or website may provide or recommendations it may make.

Please remember that Internet websites listed in this work may have changed or disappeared between when this work was written and when it is read.

Contents

Introduction

In our contemporary global landscape, replete with its vast tapestry of religious diversities and theological contentions, one institution stands as a towering edifice of spiritual truth: the Roman Catholic Church. Spanning millennia, this venerable institution is not merely an aggregation of believers or a repository of doctrine but a living, breathing manifestation of divine revelation. In this book, we endeavor to elucidate the preeminence of Roman Catholicism, inviting adherents of all world faiths to explore, engage with, and ultimately recognize the unique spiritual authority it embodies.

The Roman Catholic Church, as the "Spouse of the Holy Spirit," holds a unique and divinely instituted relationship that transcends human conceptions of temporality and materialism. It serves as a celestial bridge, a spiritual conduit through which divine grace flows to humanity. This particular union, a mystical marriage of sorts, posits the Church not as a mere facilitator but as an indispensable vehicle for salvation, sanctification, and ultimate spiritual fulfillment. As Thomas Aquinas synthesized reason and faith, and as G.K. Chesterton juxtaposed paradox with humor, our narrative intertwines scientific rigor with profound philosophical insights to present an intellectually robust yet spiritually enriching argument.

Our shared journey begins with an in-depth examination of Roman Catholicism's bedrock principles, foundational beliefs that anchor the faithful amidst the shifting sands of cultural and theological relativism. We will dissect the nature of Sacred Tradition and Sacred Scripture, exploring how these twin pillars serve not only as historical artifacts but as living, breathing elements of divine pedagogy. Through this dissection, we aim to emphasize the Church's role as both guardian and interpreter of everlasting truth.

Subsequent chapters will propel us into the transformative milieu of Vatican II, an ecclesiastical watershed that redefined modern Catholic thought and interfaith dialogue. Far from being an isolated event, Vatican II inaugurated an era of renewed engagement with the world's diverse spiritual traditions. This ecumenical council catalyzed discussions that reaffirmed the Catholic Church's commitment to dialogue, unity, and respect for other faiths, while never diluting the supremacy of Catholic doctrine.

Moreover, we'll delve into the theological underpinnings that make interfaith dialogue not only possible but fruitful. Recognizing the Church as the true Bride of Christ in an increasingly pluralistic society demands a nuanced understanding that marries theological exclusivity with pastoral inclusivity. Our exploration will tackle pressing questions like the possibility of salvation outside the Church, scrutinizing these questions through the lens of magisterial teachings and contemporary theological thought.

Of paramount importance is our extended dialogue with Protestant communities, often perceived as ideological adversaries rather than estranged brethren. We will explore shared beliefs, identify common theological ground, and confront dividing issues with intellectual honesty and doctrinal fidelity. Central to this reconciliation is a thorough examination of key doctrinal divides—pertaining to sacraments, ecclesiastical authority, and scriptural interpretation—leading us to a path of potential unity.

The schism with the Eastern Orthodox Church presents another historical and theological labyrinth. We'll navigate similarities and ritualistic differences, questioning whether the "Filioque" remains the fulcrum of division or a relic of theological semantics ripe for reconciliation. Bridging this ancient schism holds the promise of a more unified Christendom, a goal toward which our analysis will relentlessly strive.

In an age marred by rising secularism and growing atheistic sentiment, our encounters with Islam offer a fertile ground for mutual understanding and respect. By acknowledging shared Abrahamic roots and addressing theological contentions, we create a framework within which meaningful dialogue can flourish, countering secular and atheistic critiques that often misrepresent both faiths.

The Jewish-Catholic relationship serves as another cornerstone for interfaith engagement, particularly in the light of Vatican II's profound statement in "Nostra Aetate." Healing the wounds of anti-Semitism, while celebrating shared scriptures and recognizing enduring theological divergences, constitutes a task of moral and spiritual urgency—one that this book takes up with heartfelt sincerity.

Furthermore, engaging with Eastern religions such as Buddhism and Hinduism necessitates a profound respect for mystical traditions while steadfastly witnessing to Catholic truth. This intricate dance of respect and witness will be explored thoughtfully, demonstrating that the universal call to Catholicism resonates even within the spiritual frameworks of these ancient faiths.

At a time when the world fractured into countless ideological fragments, the mission of evangelization must be approached with particular sensitivity and respect. The Roman Catholic Church, envisioned as a beacon of hope, offers a moral and spiritual compass in a world adrift in relativism and nihilism. This missionary imperative is not about proselytizing with mechanical zeal but about extending an invitation rooted in love and truth.

Our exploration is not merely an academic exercise but a heartfelt appeal to engage with and embrace the spiritual richness that Roman Catholicism uniquely offers. The process of the Rite of Christian Initiation of Adults (RCIA), embedded within the very fabric of the Church's welcoming embrace, serves as a tangible pathway for those who seek deeper communion with this divine institution. This initiation process, which we will detail in the appendix, reflects the Church's commitment to inculcating faith through informed consent, catechesis, and sacramental grace.

In conclusion, the journey we embark upon is one of enlightenment, reconciliation, and profound spiritual awakening. Rooted in the traditions of the Church yet dynamically engaged with contemporary theological discourse, this text aims to be a beacon guiding all towards the luminous truth of Roman Catholicism. A harmonious blend of persuasive, scientific, and philosophical discourse, this book invites you to contemplate, challenge, and ultimately embrace a path illuminated by centuries of divine wisdom and human inquiry.

Chapter 1: The Bedrock of Belief: Roman Catholicism Defined

Roman Catholicism stands as the ancient bedrock upon which countless generations have founded their faith and morals. Its deep roots stretch back to apostolic times, forging an indelible link with the life and teachings of Jesus Christ. The Church, often referred to as the Mystical Body of Christ, represents the visible and invisible unity of all believers. It transcends time and space, uniting past, present, and future followers in a divine tapestry interwoven with sacred tradition, dogma, and the living Magisterium.

The essence of Roman Catholicism is encapsulated in both its visible and sacramental nature. Each sacrament serves as an outward sign of an inward grace, instituted by Christ for the Church's sanctification. Baptism, Eucharist, Confirmation, and others manifest the tangible touch of the divine on human existence (Catechism of the Catholic Church [CCC], 1994). The Church's sacramental life becomes the conduit through which divine life is dispensed to the faithful, marking the transformative journey from creation to redemption.

Far from being a mere institution, the Roman Catholic Church embodies a divine relationship, rooted in its self-identification as the Spouse of the Holy Spirit. This mystical union underscores the Church's mission: to guard the deposit of faith through Sacred Tradition and Sacred Scripture (Flannery, 1996). These twin pillars serve not only as a foundation for ecclesiastical authority but also as a wellspring of spiritual nourishment, guiding believers through the temporal journey towards eternal life.

Historically, the Church's outreach has stitched together a narrative of inclusivity and universal love. From the early councils to contemporary ecumenical dialogues, Catholicism has persistently sought to embrace humanity in its fullest spectrum. This historical outreach is more than a series of events; it is the ongoing testament to the Church's divine mandate to be the light of the world and the salt of the earth (Matthew 5:13-16).

In sum, Roman Catholicism isn't merely a faith tradition; it is a comprehensive worldview, a theological, philosophical, and sacramental totality that invites every soul into a journey of deeper union with God. The Church's teachings, sacraments, and divine relationships serve as beacons guiding the faithful and scholars alike towards the ultimate truth and spiritual superiority found in communion with the Roman Catholic Church.

The Spouse of the Holy Spirit: Understanding the Church's Divine Relationship

In exploring the very essence of Roman Catholicism as articulated in the broader context of "The Bedrock of Belief: Roman Catholicism Defined," we must delve deeply into the concept of the Church as the Spouse of the Holy Spirit. This profound relationship is not merely symbolic but is foundational to understanding the Church's divine mission and its role in the salvation of humanity.

The Roman Catholic Church has long been perceived as the mystical body of Christ, with a unique and intimate connection to the Holy Spirit. This relationship is vividly encapsulated in the imagery of marriage, where the Church is seen as the bride, and the Holy Spirit as the celestial spouse. This divine matrimony marks the Church's creation at Pentecost, symbolizing her spiritual fecundity and her role in bringing forth new spiritual life through the sacraments.

The metaphor of marriage is not just poetic but theologically rich. It emphasizes fidelity, unity, and an indissoluble bond. In Ephesians 5:25-27, St. Paul draws a parallel between the love of a husband for his wife and Christ's love for the Church, highlighting that Christ gave Himself up for her to make her holy. This conjugal imagery extends to the Holy Spirit, who animates and sanctifies the Church, ensuring that she remains a pure and faithful spouse (Keener, 2020).

At the very core, the Church's relationship with the Holy Spirit is rooted in the sacramental economy. The sacraments are the means through which the Holy Spirit dispenses divine life to the believers. Baptism, Confirmation, and the Eucharist manifest this divine relationship most vividly. In baptism, the faithful are born anew by water and the Holy Spirit, becoming members of the Church, the bride of Christ. Confirmation strengthens this bond, sealing the baptized with the gifts of the Holy Spirit, thus equipping them for their spiritual journey.

The indwelling of the Holy Spirit within the Church ensures her infallibility in matters of faith and morals, as articulated by the Magisterium. This divine guidance is a testament to the protective and nurturing role of the Holy Spirit, akin to a spouse who safeguards and supports (Ratzinger, 2005). The gift of infallibility, while often misunderstood, is crucial for maintaining the purity of the Church's teachings and doctrines, ensuring they are free from error, akin to the immaculate spouse as envisioned in scriptures.

Moreover, this divine relationship has ecclesiological implications that span beyond the confines of the Church's walls. The Holy Spirit's role as the spouse of the Church mandates a universal mission, embodying the Catholic (universal) aspect of Roman Catholicism. In this divine partnership, the Church is called to be a beacon of light and truth in a fragmented world, carrying forth the Holy Spirit's work of sanctification and evangelization.

Understanding this divine relationship also sheds light on the intrinsic connection between the Church and the communion of saints. The saints, as exemplars of faith, reflect the Church's fruitful union with the Holy Spirit. Their lives and intercessions testify to the transformative power of this relationship, demonstrating the Holy Spirit's perpetual action within the world through the Church.

The Spouse of the Holy Spirit also means that the Church herself partakes in the divine mission of love and redemption. This partnership is not passive; it implicates an active participation in God's salvific plan. In the spirit of conjugal unity, the Church, through her teachings, liturgy, and apostolic works, contributes to the sanctification of the world. This symbiotic relationship emphasizes the Church's active role, imbued with the Holy Spirit's dynamism, in leading the faithful towards salvation.

Furthermore, the understanding of the Church as the Spouse of the Holy Spirit provides a profound lens through which we can view her social teachings and engagements. The Church's commitment to justice, peace, and the common good reflects her fidelity to the Holy Spirit. This relationship compels the Church to act not merely as a religious institution but as a transformative agent in society, guided by the principles of righteousness and charity imparted by the Holy Spirit.

In summation, the Church's divine relationship as the Spouse of the Holy Spirit is not just a theological concept but a lived reality. It underscores the Church's identity and mission, perpetuating the transformative power of the Holy Spirit within her and through her, onto the world. The Roman Catholic Church, in her marital unity with the Holy Spirit, stands as a testament to divine love and continual guidance, embodying the ideals of spiritual fecundity, sanctity, and universal outreach.

Guardians of the Gateway: Sacred Tradition and Sacred Scripture

In the rich tapestry of Roman Catholicism, two pillars stand as the guardians of the gateway to divine understanding: Sacred Tradition and Sacred Scripture. These twin sources of revelation are not merely historical artifacts but living fonts of wisdom, perpetually guiding and shaping the faithful. They encapsulate the Church's enduring commitment to preserving and transmitting the divine truths entrusted to it from the very beginning.

Sacred Tradition, often misunderstood or overshadowed by the more widely known Sacred Scripture, is the unwritten reservoir of theological truths passed down through the generations. It comprises the beliefs, liturgical practices, and interpretations of the faith that have been perpetuated from the time of the Apostles. The Catechism of the Catholic Church (CCC) articulates this beautifully, explaining that Tradition is characterized by "the Church, in her doctrine, life, and worship, perpetuates and transmits to every generation all that she herself is, all that she believes" (CCC, 1994).

On the other hand, Sacred Scripture is the written record of God's revelation, a collection of texts inspired by the Holy Spirit and canonically recognized by the Church. The Bible, in its totality, is more than a historical document; it is the living Word of God. This bibliographic corpus encompasses the Old and New Testaments, revealing God's salvific plan through narratives, prophecies, laws, and teachings. As Pope Benedict XVI elaborated, "The Scriptures give us the divine vocabulary we need to speak about God and the human soul" (Ratzinger, 2008).

The symbiosis of Sacred Tradition and Sacred Scripture is integral to Roman Catholic theology. Neither can be fully understood in isolation, for they mutually illuminate one another. Tradition helps interpret Scripture authentically, safeguarding against misinterpretation by rooting the written Word within the broader context of the Church's historical and theological continuities. Scripture, in turn, provides the canonical foundation upon which Tradition stands. This interconnectedness was affirmed at the Second Vatican Council, which stated, "Sacred Tradition and Sacred Scripture form one sacred deposit of the word of God, committed to the Church" (Dei Verbum, 1965).

The magisterium, or teaching authority of the Church, serves as the custodian of this sacred deposit. The Pope and bishops, through their apostolic succession, have been vested with the authority to authentically interpret and teach both Tradition and Scripture. This is not a mere human authority but a divine mandate, as Jesus Christ Himself entrusted the Apostles and their successors with the mission to teach all nations (Matthew 28:19-20). Thus, the magisterium ensures doctrinal consistency and continuity, safeguarding the truth against the vicissitudes of time and culture.

It is through the interplay of Tradition, Scripture, and Magisterium that Roman Catholic teaching maintains its integrity and vitality. The magisterium's role is not to introduce new revelations but to faithfully expound the revelation already given. As Saint John Henry Newman aptly noted, the development of doctrine is a "growth in understanding, not an alteration of the essence" (Newman, 1845). This organic development allows the Church to respond to new questions and contexts without compromising the core truths of the faith.

Moreover, Sacred Tradition and Sacred Scripture serve as the bedrock for the Church's liturgical life. The liturgy, particularly the Eucharist, is a living expression of these twin sources. Every Mass is a re-presentation of the Paschal Mystery, deeply rooted in the Scriptural narrative and enriched by the Traditional practices that have evolved over centuries. The Second Vatican Council emphasized this liturgical symbiosis, declaring that "the Church has always venerated the Scriptures as she venerates the Lord's Body" (Sacrosanctum Concilium, 1963).

In recognizing the complementary nature of Sacred Tradition and Sacred Scripture, one must also appreciate their role in ecumenical dialogue. The division within Christianity, particularly between Catholicism and Protestantism, often centers on differing views regarding these sources of revelation. Protestants typically adhere to 'sola scriptura' (scripture alone), which posits Scripture as the sole authority. Conversely, Catholicism upholds the necessity of Tradition alongside Scripture, a stance rooted in the early Church's practices and the scriptural affirmation that "he who hears you hears me" (Luke 10:16).

Contemporary scholarship has increasingly acknowledged the value of Tradition in understanding the historical and cultural contexts of Scripture. Scholars like Jaroslav Pelikan have argued that "Tradition is the living faith of the dead; traditionalism is the dead faith of the living" (Pelikan, 1984). This distinction helps clarify the dynamic nature of Tradition as a living, breathing continuum, not a static relic of the past.

To facilitate a more profound engagement with Sacred Tradition and Sacred Scripture, the Church encourages the faithful to immerse themselves in both. Catechetical programs, theological seminars, and biblical studies are avenues through which believers can deepen their understanding. The Rite of Christian Initiation of Adults (RCIA) is one such example, providing a structured pathway for catechumens to explore the richness of the faith. The RCIA process is deeply rooted in Scripture and Tradition, guiding new converts through the liturgical and doctrinal landscapes of Catholicism.

In conclusion, Sacred Tradition and Sacred Scripture are not just historical legacies but living realities that continuously nourish and sustain the Roman Catholic Church. They are the twin guardians of the gateway to divine truth, interwoven seamlessly by the magisterium's interpretive authority. Together, they form the bedrock upon which the faith is built, a foundation that has withstood the test of time and will continue to guide the faithful towards the ultimate truth—the divine revelation of God in Jesus Christ.

Embracing the Other: Catholicism's Historical Outreach

The grandeur of Roman Catholicism lies not only in its rich theological heritage and doctrinal stability but also in its proactive engagement with diverse cultures and religious traditions throughout history. This outreach is not merely a tactical expansion but is rooted deeply in the Church's understanding of its mission as the custodian of divine truth and the conduit of God's grace to all humanity (McBrien, 2006). In examining the broad sweep of Catholicism's historical outreach, we witness a nuanced dance of respect, cultural integration, and unwavering proclamation of truth.

From the earliest days of the apostolic missions, the Church has seen itself as a universal sacrament—a visible sign instituted by Christ to bring all people into communion with God. St. Paul's journeys, chronicled in the Acts of the Apostles, set the precedent not only for vast geographical outreach but for engaging with diverse groups ranging from Greek philosophers to Roman centurions. These efforts underscore a pattern: engagement leads to enrichment, both for the community being evangelized and for the Church itself.

Medieval Christendom provides a mosaic of how Catholicism interacted with the multiplicity of European cultures. The Benedictine missions to England, led by figures like St.

Augustine of Canterbury, are exemplary. Pope Gregory the Great's instructions to these missionaries were explicit: respect the cultural customs of the local populations while gently integrating Christian doctrine and practice. This approach of adaptation rather than imposition showcased an early form of inculturation—adopting local customs into the Christian liturgical framework, thereby making Christianity more accessible while maintaining doctrinal purity (Duffy, 1997).

In the discovery of the New World, the Church was again at the forefront of engagement with non-European cultures. The encomienda system, though fraught with exploitation, also paved the way for evangelization. Spanish missionaries, such as Bartolomé de las Casas, advocated vigorously for the rights of indigenous people, blending social justice with the proclamation of faith. This reveals a vision of Catholic outreach that marries evangelization with human dignity, a theme that reverberates through modern Catholic Social Teaching.

Moving into the modern era, Vatican II (1962-1965) marks a pivotal moment in the Church's approach to other faiths and cultures. The Council's document "Nostra Aetate" (Declaration on the Relation of the Church with Non-Christian Religions) signifies a watershed in the Roman Catholic theological landscape. It calls for the recognition and respect of truths in other religions while also affirming Christianity's ultimate claim to truth through Jesus Christ. This dialectic between affirmation of truth and respect for the 'other' characterizes the sophisticated balance the Church aims to achieve in its outreach efforts.

The outreach to Islam, beginning in the medieval period with St. Francis of Assisi's encounter with Sultan Malik al-Kamil, demonstrates an early example of respectful interfaith dialogue. Francis did not seek to proselytize aggressively but instead engaged in mutual dialogue that honored the dignity of the other while remaining firm in his own faith. This model rolls forward into today's interfaith dialogues spearheaded by modern popes, including Pope John Paul II's papal visits to Islamic nations and his landmark gathering of diverse religious leaders in Assisi for a World Day of Prayer for Peace (Jørgensen, 2008).

With Judaism, the Church's relationship has evolved significantly over centuries. From the fraught and often violent interactions of the medieval and early modern periods to the post-Holocaust reconciliation efforts, Catholicism has sought to embrace its elder sibling in faith. Vatican II's "Nostra Aetate" again is instrumental, foregrounding the shared spiritual heritage and God's irrevocable covenant with the Jewish people. This stance reorients the Church's outreach, pivoting from proselytization to a shared witness to monotheism and social justice.

In Eastern contexts, Catholicism's interaction is characterized by a deep respect for the mystical and philosophical traditions of Hinduism and Buddhism. Jesuit missions in the 16th and 17th centuries led by figures such as Matteo Ricci in China and Robert de Nobili in India showcase a profound engagement that goes beyond mere conversion efforts. These missionaries immersed themselves in local culture and intellectual traditions, displaying a genuine respect for the wisdom present while simultaneously offering the Christian message. This model of outreach—dialogical, respectful, and intellectually robust—continues to inform contemporary engagements with Eastern religions.

More recently, the Church's outreach has increasingly emphasized dialogue over conversion, particularly in pluralistic societies. The approach has been one of witnessing to the truth of the Gospel through acts of love, justice, and peace, reflecting Pope Paul VI's notion that "modern man listens more willingly to witnesses than to teachers" ("Evangelii Nuntiandi", 1975). Such an approach invites a reciprocal enrichment: Catholicism grows in understanding through its encounters, and it offers its wellspring of theological, philosophical, and ethical riches to the world.

Catholic outreach is also keenly aware of the challenges posed by secularism and atheism, especially in the West. Pope Benedict XVI's speeches often highlighted the importance of reason in faith in dialogues with secular thinkers, positing that faith and reason are not mutually exclusive but are complementary. His address at the University of Regensburg in 2006, though controversial, was a pivotal moment in emphasizing the need for a reasoned dialogue with a secular world—a world increasingly distanced from transcendental concerns.

Additionally, the Roman Catholic outreach has always been characterized by a blend of pastoral care and intellectual engagement. Institutions like the Pontifical Council for Interreligious Dialogue and the various synods and commissions established post-Vatican II work tirelessly to foster mutual understanding while remaining committed to the evangelizing mission of the Church. The impulse is not just to understand but to authentically and lovingly invite others into the fold of salvation history as understood by Catholic teaching.

In conclusion, Catholicism's historical outreach is a testament to the Church's dual mission of fidelity to the Deposit of Faith and responsiveness to the human condition across diverse cultural and religious landscapes. It stands as an exemplar of how embracing the 'other' enriches the Church, enriches the world, and manifests the fullness of God's love and truth. Through this relentless pursuit of engagement, the Roman Catholic Church continues to illuminate the path to salvation, inviting all humanity to engage with its profound mysteries and divine heritage.

Chapter 2: Vatican II: A Watershed Moment for Interfaith Dialogue

The Second Vatican Council, commonly known as Vatican II, marked an unprecedented evolution in the Roman Catholic Church's approach to interfaith dialogue. Convened by Pope John XXIII between 1962 and 1965, the council aimed to address various issues confronting the Church in the contemporary world, including its relationship with other religions. This epoch-making event fundamentally reshaped the Church's stance towards other faith communities, emphasizing dialogue, collaboration, and mutual respect.

One of the most profound ways Vatican II altered interfaith dynamics was through the promulgation of the document *Nostra Aetate*. This declaration broadened the scope of the Church's interaction with people of other religions, entreating Catholics to respect and acknowledge the spiritual truths present in other faith traditions. Importantly, it underscored a shared human quest for meaning and ultimate truth. This move wasn't merely a gesture of goodwill; it was a deep theological affirmation of the inherent dignity of every human person as a seeker of divine truth (Flannery, 1996).

Moreover, *Nostra Aetate* paid special attention to Jewish-Catholic relations, denouncing all forms of anti-Semitism and encouraging mutual understanding and respect. This was a significant departure from centuries of strained relations and laid a foundation for meaningful reconciliation. The declaration acknowledged that "the Church cannot forget that she received the revelation of the Old Testament via that people with whom God in His inexpressible mercy concluded the Ancient Covenant" (*Nostra Aetate*, 1965). This acknowledgement catalyzed numerous interfaith initiatives aimed at healing old wounds and fostering new dialogue pathways (Oesterreicher, 1971).

Among the transformative outcomes of Vatican II in interfaith dialogue was the emphasis on religious freedom as delineated in *Dignitatis Humanae*. This document articulated the Church's respect for the freedom of individuals and communities to practice their religion without coercion. It marked a pivotal shift from a predominantly exclusivist stance to one that recognized the right of all people to religious self-determination. The Council reasoned that true faith cannot be compelled, highlighting an intrinsic Catholic belief in the freedom of conscience and religious expression (Murray, 1966).

Academically, Vatican II has been an abundant field of study for theologians and scholars of interfaith relations. Its influence has permeated various dimensions of theological discourse and ecclesial practice. Notably, Vatican II underscored the necessity for constructive dialogue grounded in genuine respect and intellectual rigor. Scholars such as Karl Rahner and Yves Congar have highlighted how the council's teachings necessitate engaging with other faiths not solely for conversion but to enrich theological understanding and deepen one's own faith (Ratzinger, 2005).

In contemporary practice, the vision cast by Vatican II continues to inspire and challenge. Interfaith initiatives today draw from its principles, fostering environments where dialogue thrives over discord. The Council's call for engagement rather than isolation resonates profoundly in today's pluralistic societies. To fulfill Vatican II's vision in the current era, Catholics and interfaith scholars alike must continue to pursue dialogue with humility and openness, always guided by the principles of charity and truth.

In summary, Vatican II's proclamation was a watershed moment that charted new courses in the realm of interfaith dialogue. Its progressive documents, especially *Nostra Aetate* and *Dignitatis Humanae*, broke fresh ground, setting the stage for a more inclusive and respectful rapport among world religions. As the Church moves forward, the Council's teachings remain a pivotal reference, urging a commitment to dialogue, understanding, and peace.

The Legacy of Vatican II on Modern Catholic Thought

In the annals of Church history, few events have exerted as profound an influence on modern Catholic thought as the Second Vatican Council, commonly known as Vatican II. The Council, which convened from 1962 to 1965, marked a pivotal moment, steering the Church towards new theological and pastoral engagements both internally and with the broader, ever-diversifying world. Its ramifications have permeated various aspects of Catholic doctrine, reshaping centuries-old perspectives and challenging the faithful to consider their beliefs in the light of contemporary realities.

Foremost among Vatican II's legacies is its impact on the Church's approach to interfaith dialogue. Prior to Vatican II, the Catholic Church often maintained a defensive stance towards other religions. The council's documents, especially the *Nostra Aetate*, emphasized the importance of dialogue and understanding among different faith traditions. This groundbreaking shift invited Catholics to see the Church not as an isolated citadel of truth but as an inclusive community called to witness and engage with the religious other on common moral and humanitarian grounds. The spirit of *Nostra Aetate* continues to inspire Catholic theologians and laity alike in their interactions with non-Christian traditions (Abbot, 1966).

Modern Catholic thought owes a significant portion of its contemporary ethos to Vatican II's renewed emphasis on the role of the laity. Historically, ecclesiastical functions were dominated by the clergy, leaving laity with limited spiritual roles outside liturgical attendance and moral adherence. Vatican II's *Lumen Gentium* and *Gaudium et Spes* documents articulated a more participatory ecclesiology, recognizing the laity's essential contributions to the Church's mission in the world. This recognition has led to greater lay involvement in various ministries and social justice endeavors. Theologically, it has democratized the understanding of the mystical Body of Christ, affirming the spiritual equality and vocational dignity of all baptized members of the Church (Flannery, 1996).

Another profound legacy of Vatican II on modern Catholic thought is its theological openness and emphasis on aggiornamento (updating). This theological renewal invites Catholics to engage critically yet faithfully with contemporary issues, ranging from bioethics and environmental concerns to social justice and economic inequality. The Council's innovative theological frameworks expanded the Church's intellectual horizons, fostering dialogues with secular philosophies and sciences, thus promoting a more holistic understanding of the human condition. This intellectual openness is not a departure but a deepening of Thomistic principles, rooted in reason and faith's synergy, emphasizing truth's pursuit in all its dimensions (Ratzinger, 2005).

Liturgical reforms initiated by Vatican II have also left an indelible mark on Catholic worship and spirituality. The transition from Latin to the vernacular made the liturgy more accessible, facilitating deeper congregational participation. Theologically, this change underscores the incarnational aspect of Catholic worship where the divine grace integrates into the lived experiences of the faithful. These liturgical changes are not mere ritual modifications; they are profound theological statements about God's proximity and the Church's mission to be a sacrament of salvation to the world. Modern Catholic thought continues to grapple with and celebrate these liturgical transformations, finding new expressions of ancient truths in contemporary forms of worship.

Moreover, Vatican II's endorsement of religious liberty redefined the Church's relationship with the modern state and individual conscience. The *Dignitatis Humanae* declaration affirmed the right of every person to religious freedom, a principle that had far-reaching theological and pastoral implications. This commitment to religious liberty has become a cornerstone in contemporary Catholic thought, informing the Church's stance on human rights and its advocacy for persecuted religious communities globally. It represents a move away from a triumphalist posture to one that seeks to coexist in a pluralistic world while simultaneously upholding the universal call to truth (Murray, 1966).

The council's pastoral constitution *Gaudium et Spes* laid the groundwork for what has been labeled "Catholic Social Teaching." This body of social doctrine emphasizes the Church's obligation to address the conditions of the modern world, particularly regarding issues of justice, peace, and the dignity of human labor. By placing these temporal concerns within a theological framework emphasizing the inherent dignity of every human person, Vatican II profoundly influenced how modern Catholics perceive and act upon issues of social justice. This legacy has given rise to numerous Church-sponsored initiatives and organizations dedicated to social causes, perpetuating a more socially aware and active Catholic presence in the world (Weigel, 1992).

Even as Vatican II opened windows to the world, it did not undermine the centrality of traditional doctrines but offered them renewed vigor and relevance. Prominent theologians like Karl Rahner and Henri de Lubac found themselves navigating ancient doctrines through the prism of modern existential and cultural questions, reaffirming their timelessness while exploring their contemporary applications. Thus, Vatican II's legacy in modern Catholic thought includes the dynamic tension of maintaining doctrinal orthodoxy while engaging openly with the complexities of the human experience.

In sum, the legacy of Vatican II on modern Catholic thought is multifaceted and profound. It ushered in a renewed understanding of interfaith dialogue, expanded the role of the laity, embraced theological openness, reformed liturgical practices, affirmed religious liberty, emphasized social justice, and reaffirmed traditional doctrines in a modern context. This legacy continues to shape the faith and practice of contemporary Catholics, challenging them to live out their beliefs with renewed vigor and relevance in a rapidly changing world. As we move further into the 21st century, Vatican II remains a beacon, guiding Catholics toward a deeper, more inclusive, and engaged faith.

Implementing Vatican II's Vision in Today's World

The vision of Vatican II, particularly in the realm of interfaith dialogue, offers a robust framework that continues to guide the Roman Catholic Church. The Council, held from 1962 to 1965, marked a critical juncture in modern Catholic thought, heralding an era of engagement and dialogue rather than confrontation and isolation. But how does one translate the seismic shifts in ecclesiastical approach promoted by Vatican II into actionable steps in the 21st century?

Implementing Vatican II's vision demands a deep, revised understanding of what it means to engage with other faith traditions in a globalized, pluralistic society. The operative principles derived from key documents such as *Nostra Aetate*, *Gaudium et Spes*, and *Lumen Gentium* provide fertile ground for fostering interreligious harmony and mutual respect. These texts emphasize that while the Roman Catholic Church holds fast to its doctrinal truths, it must also seek to understand and appreciate the religious experience of others (Flannery, 1996).

To commence this implementation effectively, one must first recognize the evolving nature of religious identity. In contemporary society, individuals increasingly view their faith as a personal journey rather than a static affiliation.

Consequently, the Church's role is dual-faceted: to witness its own profound truths while also becoming a listener and learner in the myriad dialogues it engages in. One cannot overlook the necessity for the Church to present itself not as an adversary but as a companion seeking shared understanding.

This posture of active listening and mutual respect requires theological grounding. According to the teachings of Vatican II, every human possesses an inherent dignity and a capacity for seeking truth and goodness. This anthropological perspective serves as an excellent starting point for interfaith dialogue. By respecting each person's inherent dignity, the Church can engage meaningfully with individuals from different religious backgrounds. *Lumen Gentium* speaks to this inclusivity by noting that the Church serves as a light to all nations, a beacon that draws people towards divine truth (Vatican Council II, 1964).

Yet, implementing this vision in the real world often encounters the obstacles of misconceptions and stereotypes. Both within and outside the Church, people may harbor biases that fuel mistrust and division. Thus, educational programs aimed at debunking myths and promoting accurate understandings of different religions become invaluable. The Church has a responsibility to educate its faithful about the theological and cultural richness of other faith traditions. This education must go beyond mere tolerance, moving towards genuine appreciation and respect, something John Paul II fervently advocated during his papacy.

A practical step towards realizing Vatican II's vision is the institution of spaces for dialogue—both physical and metaphorical. These could range from interfaith councils and symposiums to more localized initiatives like community centers or parish-based discussion groups. These spaces should not only focus on theological discourse but also on shared community concerns, such as social justice, environmental stewardship, and ethical business practices. By collaborating on common causes, shared values become evident, fortifying bonds between different religious communities.

Moreover, the Church must leverage modern technology to expand its outreach. In this digital age, online forums, social media platforms, and virtual conferences provide unparalleled opportunities for interfaith engagement. The Pope's regular use of Twitter, for instance, exemplifies how the Church can project its message of peace and unity to a broader audience. These digital tools also facilitate real-time dialogues, making it easier to share experiences, ideas, and solutions across geographic boundaries.

Alongside these institutional measures, there is a crucial need for leadership that embodies the spirit of Vatican II. Clergy and laity alike must be trained to act as ambassadors of this vision. This requires a renewed emphasis in seminary and theological education on the principles of interfaith dialogue, as delineated in Vatican II documents. By shaping future leaders who are both firmly rooted in Catholic doctrine and open to respectful exchanges with other faiths, the Church can ensure that its vision is both upheld and advanced.

The implementation of Vatican II's vision is not solely the purview of Church authorities—it is a communal endeavor. Lay participation is essential in substantively embedding this vision into everyday practices. Programs for the laity that focus on developing an understanding of Vatican II principles and imparting practical skills for dialogue can prove transformative. By equipping ordinary Catholics with the tools to engage constructively with those of other faiths, the Church becomes a living testament to its own ideals.

Discussing these concepts in educational institutions is another vital arena for implementation. University courses that incorporate Vatican II's teachings within broader academic curricula offer students a scholarly yet faith-informed approach to interfaith engagement. This not only aids in dispelling ignorance but also fosters an environment where intellectual and spiritual exploration can coexist harmoniously.

Another dimension often overlooked is the incorporation of Vatican II's vision into the arts and culture. The Church has historically been a patron of the arts, and this avenue can once again serve a pivotal role. Art, music, literature, and film that reflect the themes of unity, peace, and mutual respect can transcend doctrinal differences and touch hearts in ways that dialogue alone cannot. Initiatives like interfaith art exhibitions or music festivals can serve as bridges between communities, fostering a spirit of communal celebration and understanding.

Finally, it is imperative to acknowledge the complexity of modern global issues and how they impact interfaith relations. Topics like migration, economic inequality, and climate change necessitate a collaborative response from religious communities and the Church must be an active participant in these discussions. Vatican II emphasized the Church's commitment to social justice, and today's world demands that this commitment extends beyond denominational lines. Cooperation on these fronts serves as a tangible manifestation of the unity and mutual respect advocated by Vatican II.

The Church's mission, illuminated and rejuvenated by Vatican II, requires both contemplative understanding and dynamic action.

The call to engagement is not a temporary endeavor but a continuous journey. As we strive to implement Vatican II's vision in today's world, we build not just a more inclusive Church but also a more compassionate and united global community.

Chapter 3: Theological Foundations for Interfaith Engagement

Interfaith engagement has become an essential endeavor in our globalized world, particularly for the Roman Catholic Church. This undertaking is not merely pragmatic but deeply rooted in the theological heritage of Catholicism. The Second Vatican Council established a more inclusive and open approach towards other faiths while maintaining the Church's commitment to its doctrinal truths. This chapter aims to elucidate the theological principles that allow for genuine interfaith dialogue, asserting the importance of recognizing the Roman Catholic Church as the true vessel of salvation.

At the heart of interfaith engagement lies the concept of the "Church as the Body of Christ" (Lumen Gentium, 1964). This ecclesiological vision mandates that the Church is not an isolated community but a universal body called to engage with all humanity. Vatican II's declaration "Nostra Aetate" broadened the horizon for interfaith discussions, emphasizing the shared search for divine truth and moral guidance among world religions. The appreciation of authentic spiritual values in other religious traditions creates a fertile ground for mutual respect and understanding (Nostra Aetate, 1965).

The notion of "anonymous Christians," a term popularized by theologian Karl Rahner, further underscores the possibility of salvation outside the visible boundaries of the Church. Rahner posited that individuals who lived according to the morals and truths of Christianity, albeit unknowingly, were in an implicit relationship with the Church (Rahner, 1966). Such a perspective fosters a compassionate and inclusive stance, conducive to genuine dialogue and mutual enrichment.

However, it is imperative to assert that while the Church acknowledges elements of truth and holiness in other religions, this does not equate to seeing all religions as equally valid. The Church firmly believes in its unique role as the "sacrament of salvation" (Henrici, 2003). As Pope John Paul II noted, "Dialogue does not originate from tactical concerns or self-interest, but is an activity with its own guiding principles, requirements, and dignity" (Redemptoris Missio, 1990).

The principle of "subsistit in" from Lumen Gentium serves as a cornerstone for understanding the Church's relation to other faiths. By stating that the true Church of Christ "subsists in" the Catholic Church, it allows for the existence of ecclesial elements in other communities (Gaillardetz, 2005). This complex yet profound theology opens the door for recognizing genuine spiritual experiences outside the Catholic faith while affirming the fullness of revelation within the Church.

To promote fruitful interfaith engagement, the Church must rely on two principal virtues: humility and charity. Humility allows Catholics to approach other religions with an openness to learn and a readiness to acknowledge the working of the Holy Spirit beyond one's understanding. Charity, on the other hand, ensures that dialogue is always pursued with the best interests of the other, aiming for mutual growth and understanding, not mere conversion or dominance. Without these virtues, interfaith dialogue can devolve into prideful disputes rather than genuine encounters.

This chapter has shown that the theological foundations for interfaith engagement are deeply embedded in the Roman Catholic tradition, affirming the Church's unique role in the divine plan while fostering a genuine and respectful dialogue with adherents of other faiths. As we move forward in this discussion, it is crucial to maintain this dual commitment to truth and openness, ensuring that the Roman Catholic Church continues to be both a witness of Christ's love and a beacon of hope in an increasingly pluralistic world.

Recognizing the True Bride of Christ in a Pluralistic Society

In today's world, characterized by unprecedented global interconnectivity and a multiplicity of religious traditions, the quest to identify the true Bride of Christ may appear daunting. However, for Roman Catholics, this recognition is both a matter of faith and a reasoned conclusion grounded in theological reflection. The assertion that the Roman Catholic Church is the true Bride of Christ, the one holy, catholic, and apostolic Church, stands as a fundamental belief deriving from Christ's own institution.

The theological underpinnings for identifying the true Bride of Christ are deeply rooted in scripture and tradition. According to Ephesians 5:25-27, Christ loved the Church and gave himself up for her to make her holy, cleansing her with the washing of water through the word. This description provides a framework for understanding the special bond between Christ and His Church, a bond manifest primarily in the Roman Catholic Church through its sacraments, teachings, and hierarchical structure (Catechism of the Catholic Church, 1997). The sacramental life of the Church, particularly the Eucharist, is viewed as both the source and the summit of Christian life, making visible the invisible reality of Christ's presence (Sacrosanctum Concilium, 1963).

Amidst a pluralistic society, the Church does not deny the partial truths and goodness present in other religions. Instead, it acknowledges that these elements can serve as a preparation for the Gospel (Nostra Aetate, 1965). Yet, this acknowledgment does not dilute the Church's self-understanding as the Bride of Christ. Rather, it strengthens the call to engage in respectful dialogue grounded in the Church's confidence in its own identity and mission. Dialogue begins from the premise of seeking truth together, holding that the fullness of divine revelation is preserved uniquely in the Roman Catholic tradition (Lumen Gentium, 1964).

This inclusive approach does not relativize truth but points to the complementarity of faith and reason. In a pluralistic society, the Church upholds universality without compromising the particularity of Christ's revelation. The Church's magisterium, understood as the teaching authority instituted by Christ through the apostles, ensures the integrity and continuity of this revelation (Dei Verbum, 1965). Accordingly, full adherence to the Church means embracing its teachings on faith and morals, articulated through this apostolic succession.

While other religious traditions may offer profound spiritual experiences and ethical insights, it is within the Roman Catholic Church that the fullness of Christian revelation subsists, making her the Bride of Christ. This claim is not intended to diminish the sincerity of believers in other faiths but to invite them to consider the wholeness of Catholic truth. Vatican II opened new pathways for mutual understanding, compassion, and respect, while maintaining that only in Christ can the mystery of human existence find true illumination (Gaudium et Spes, 1965).

In practical terms, the process of discerning and recognizing the true Bride of Christ involves an engagement with the Church's sacramental life, a study of its doctrines, and an experience of its communal worship. The Rite of Christian Initiation of Adults (RCIA) serves as the primary pathway for those coming from other religious backgrounds. Through RCIA, individuals undergo a systematic journey of faith formation, which culminates in reception into the Church and full participation in its sacramental life (Appendix A).

As the Church reaches out to other faith communities, it also underscores the notion of grace operative outside its visible boundaries. The Church holds that salvation is ultimately possible for all, even those who, through no fault of their own, do not know Christ and his Church. However, this openness does not negate the Church's mission to evangelize, proclaiming that it is in the Catholic Church that the means of salvation are fully accessible (Ad Gentes, 1965).

In conclusion, recognizing the true Bride of Christ in a pluralistic society calls for a theological discernment rooted in faith and reason, a respectful engagement with other religions, and a commitment to proclaim the unique fullness of truth found in the Roman Catholic Church. This recognition is a testament to the Church's divine foundation and its mission to lead all people to the fullness of life in Christ.

Salvation Outside the Church? A Catholic Perspective

The question of salvation outside the Roman Catholic Church has long been a subject of theological debate and contemplation. This issue is particularly pertinent in the context of interfaith engagement, where understanding and respect for other beliefs are crucial. Roman Catholic theology, deeply rooted in both sacred tradition and sacred scripture, provides a compelling framework for navigating these complex waters.

From a historical perspective, the Roman Catholic Church has traditionally held the stance of "extra Ecclesiam nulla salus" or "outside the Church, there is no salvation" (Fenton, 1958). This phrase, originating from early Church Fathers like Cyprian of Carthage, emphasizes the Church's critical role in mediating God's grace to humanity. Yet, this doctrine has evolved, especially in the light of the Second Vatican Council, which brought new depth and nuance to the understanding of interfaith relations.

Vatican II's document "Lumen Gentium" made significant strides in broadening the concept of salvation. It acknowledges that those who, through no fault of their own, do not know the gospel of Christ or His Church but seek God with a sincere heart may also achieve salvation (Paul VI, 1964). This shift is monumental, suggesting that God's grace is not confined solely within the institutional boundaries of the Church. Instead, it recognizes the validity of other spiritual paths and the sincerity of those who seek truth and goodness.

Interestingly, "Lumen Gentium" is not an outright abandonment of the traditional stance but rather an expansion. It positions the Church as a universal sacrament of salvation, implying that while the fullness of truth resides in the Roman Catholic Church, elements of that very same truth may be found in other religious traditions (Paul VI, 1964). This understanding forms the basis for the Church's interfaith engagement, allowing Catholics to respect other religions while holding firm to their belief in the Church's unique salvific role.

Philosophically, this raises intriguing questions about the nature of truth and salvation. How do we reconcile the Church's claim to be the true Bride of Christ with a pluralistic world filled with diverse religious expressions? The answer lies, perhaps, in the very nature of God's self-revelation. Thomas Aquinas, in his synthesis of faith and reason, emphasizes that God's truth can be apprehended by human reason, yet fully comprehended only through divine revelation (Aquinas, Summa Theologica I, q. 16, a. 1). This suggests that while elements of divine truth can manifest in varied religious contexts, the complete revelation is found in Christ and His Church.

Aquinas' theological insights are essential for understanding the Catholic perspective on salvation outside the Church. He posits that all truth is God's truth, thus recognizing the seeds of the Word (logoi spermatikoi) planted in other cultures and religions (Aquinas, Summa Theologica I, q. 12, a. 13). These seeds of truth foster a natural openness toward finding common ground in interfaith dialogues, making the Church's outreach more effective and respectful.

The practical implications of this nuanced stance on salvation are profound for interfaith engagement. This theological foundation allows Catholics to engage with members of other religions in a spirit of shared humanity and mutual respect while affirming their own faith's truths. Catholic theologians and scholars play a crucial role here, formulating and disseminating a balanced understanding that bridges doctrinal integrity with dialogue.

Moreover, the Church's interfaith endeavors must be aligned with its mission of evangelization. This mission isn't about coercion but inviting others into the fullness of Christ's truth as cherished by the Church. In line with Chesterton's view, the Church should present its beliefs not as a monolithic demand but as a profound invitation - an invitation to witness to the richness and depth of the Gospel (Chesterton, 1925). Respectful, loving witness is key in promoting understanding and potentially leading others to explore the Catholic faith.

Furthermore, the Rite of Christian Initiation of Adults (RCIA) reflects the Church's commitment to guiding converts with patience and respect, addressing their unique backgrounds and prior spiritual journeys. This process can be seen as both an expression of the Church's inclusivity and a testament to its belief in its mission to share the fullness of Christ's truth.

In theological discussions, the notion of "baptism by desire" is also crucial. According to Church teaching, even those who, without formal baptism, sincerely seek what is right and live according to their understanding of God's will, may be saved (Catechism of the Catholic Church, 1994). This concept resonates deeply with Vatican II's inclusive vision and emphasizes God's mercy and justice.

However, while the Church's openness towards other paths of faith demonstrates a spirit of inclusivity, it does not negate the Church's belief in its unique role in salvation history. Catholic doctrine upholds that the sacraments, particularly the Eucharist, are vital means of grace that the Church alone can fully administer (Martos, 2001). This asserts the Church's indispensable role while fostering an environment where interfaith dialogues can flourish without compromising Catholic integrity.

Ultimately, the Roman Catholic Church today stands at an intersection of tradition and modernity, firmly grounded in its historical doctrines while dynamically engaging with the reality of a diverse, multi-religious world. This balance is not merely a strategic necessity but a theological imperative, rooted in the conviction that the path to salvation, while uniquely embodied in the Church, can be illuminated by the rays of truth found in many places.

For interfaith scholars and theologians alike, this perspective offers fertile ground for exploration and dialogue, pushing the boundaries of how we understand divine revelation, human salvation, and the role of the Church in a pluralistic world. The Catholic Church thus embraces its mission with both humility and confidence, inviting all people to a deeper encounter with the transformative love of Christ.

Chapter 4: Engaging Protestant "Heretics": A Path to Reconciliation

Protestant communities, often called "heretics" in historical Roman Catholic discourse, have played a significant role in shaping the religious landscape since the Reformation. The term itself is laden with contention, but as we move further into the modern era, it becomes imperative for the Roman Catholic Church to engage Protestant groups in meaningful dialogue. This chapter explores the underpinnings of such engagements with the aim of fostering reconciliation and returning to a shared spiritual heritage.

First, one must consider the areas of common ground between Catholicism and Protestantism. Both traditions adhere to core Christian beliefs, such as the Trinity, the divinity of Christ, and the sanctity of the Scriptures. These shared convictions serve as a foundation for dialogue and potential unity. However, the sincerity and depth of this common ground should not be merely academic but lived through genuine respect and understanding. Engaging in conversations about shared beliefs demonstrates goodwill and paves the way for addressing deeper doctrinal divides.

The most contentious issues often revolve around sacraments, authority, and interpretation of Scripture. Sacramental theology within Catholicism emphasizes the seven sacraments as channels of grace instituted by Christ. In contrast, many Protestant communities recognize only two or none, leading to theological friction. These differences are not merely academic but impact diverse aspects of religious life, from baptism to the Eucharist (Schillebeeckx, 1985). Clarifying these views with theological rigor and empathy can highlight the profound intentions behind each sacramental practice.

Authority within the Church is another critical divide. The Catholic Church's hierarchical structure, with the Pope deemed as the successor of St. Peter, contrasts sharply with the often decentralized Protestant governance. This divergence raises questions about interpretative authority, which extends to the interpretation of the Scriptures themselves. The principle of *sola scriptura* (scripture alone) embraced by many Protestants stands in opposition to the Catholic reliance on both Sacred Scripture and Sacred Tradition (Catechism of the Catholic Church, 1994). Bridging this gap necessitates an appreciation for the historical contexts in which these doctrines arose while envisioning a future that can accommodate mutual respect.

In addressing these theological divides, the Second Vatican Council's (1962-1965) commitment to ecumenism provides a blueprint. The Council encouraged Catholics to engage in dialogue with other Christian communities, stressing that "elements of sanctification and of truth" are present in them (Lumen Gentium, 1964). This directive fosters not just tolerance but proactive engagement, urging Catholics to encounter Protestants as co-pilgrims rather than adversaries. By understanding the historical grievances and theological distinctions, Catholics can better approach conversations that do not dwell merely on differences but seek actionable paths to unity.

Practical steps towards reconciliation can take many forms, from academic conferences to local community initiatives. Creating platforms for theological dialogue is essential. Yet, equally vital are grassroots efforts where Catholics and Protestants come together to serve their communities, participate in joint prayer services, and learn from each other's traditions. These engagements humanize theological discussions and frame them within lived experiences.

In conclusion, engaging with Protestant communities should not be perceived as a task of converting the "heretics" but as an enriching interaction that might bridge centuries-old divides. It involves recognizing profound shared roots and addressing discrepancies with humility and intellectual honesty. By fostering such engagements, the Roman Catholic Church

reaffirms its commitment to unity under the broader umbrella
of Christian truth.

Common Ground: Shared Beliefs with Protestant Communities

In the endeavor to engage with our Protestant brethren, it is crucial to identify and celebrate the common ground we share. While doctrinal differences have long divided Roman Catholics and Protestants, many fundamental beliefs unite us. These shared convictions serve as a solid foundation for mutual understanding and collaboration, fostering a spirit of reconciliation and furthering the greater cause of Christian unity.

First and foremost, both Roman Catholics and Protestants profess faith in Jesus Christ as the Son of God and the Savior of humanity. This Christological consensus forms the cornerstone of our shared Christian identity. By affirming Christ's divine nature and redemptive mission, we acknowledge our common dedication to following His teachings and striving to live in accordance with His example.

Furthermore, the concept of the Holy Trinity is another significant area of agreement. Both traditions uphold the belief in one God manifesting in three distinct persons: the Father, the Son, and the Holy Spirit. This Trinitarian doctrine is central to understanding God's nature and His work in the world. Though nuances in the interpretation of the Trinity might vary, the core belief remains a strong unifying factor.

Another key doctrinal convergence is the authority of Sacred Scripture. Both Roman Catholics and Protestants view the Bible as the inspired Word of God, containing the truth necessary for salvation and moral guidance. While the Catholic Church additionally relies on Sacred Tradition, the shared reverence for Holy Scripture establishes a critical commonality. The Bible serves as a mutual guiding text, encouraging both communities to delve deeper into its messages and derive spiritual enrichment.

The sacrament of baptism represents an additional shared tradition, symbolizing entry into the Christian faith. Both Roman Catholic and Protestant communities administer baptism as a rite of initiation, cleansing the individual of original sin and marking the beginning of a new life in Christ. This sacramental bond underscores our collective commitment to welcoming new members into the Christian fold, emphasizing the transformative power of God's grace.

Moreover, the shared belief in the necessity of grace for salvation is a crucial aspect of our common ground. Both traditions recognize human incapacity to attain salvation through works alone, underscoring the indispensability of divine grace. This shared emphasis on grace highlights our mutual dependence on God's benevolence and reaffirms our trust in His mercy and love for humanity.

The principle of loving one's neighbor as oneself, derived from Christ's teachings, is another area where Roman Catholics and Protestants find commonality. Both communities advocate for living lives characterized by compassion, kindness, and social justice. This ethical commitment to serving others and addressing societal injustices exemplifies our shared mission to embody Christ's love in the world.

In addition to theological and ethical commonalities, there are practical similarities in worship practices. Both Roman Catholics and Protestants gather for regular worship services, involving prayer, hymn-singing, and preaching. These communal gatherings reflect our shared dedication to fostering fellowship and worshiping God collectively, providing opportunities for mutual edification and spiritual growth.

The acknowledgment of the Apostles' Creed and the Nicene Creed is another unifying element. These ancient creeds encapsulate the foundational beliefs of Christianity, summarizing key tenets of the faith. Both Roman Catholics and many Protestant denominations recite these creeds, affirming their adherence to the historic truths of Christianity. This common liturgical heritage strengthens our bonds and reinforces our shared doctrinal foundation.

Furthermore, both communities hold a high regard for the moral teachings of Jesus, particularly those articulated in the Sermon on the Mount. The Beatitudes and the call to righteousness resonate deeply within both traditions, inspiring a commitment to ethical living and spiritual integrity. These teachings provide a collective moral compass, guiding both Roman Catholics and Protestants in their personal and communal lives.

It is essential to acknowledge that the quest for social justice unites both traditions. From feeding the hungry to advocating for the marginalized, Roman Catholics and Protestants often find themselves on the front lines of humanitarian efforts. These shared actions toward bettering society embody Christ's command to love and serve one another, breaking down barriers and promoting unity through common purpose.

A profound example of common theological ground lies in the concept of the "priesthood of all believers." While Roman Catholicism maintains an ordained priesthood, the idea that all baptized Christians share in Christ's priestly mission finds resonance in both traditions. This shared belief empowers lay members to actively participate in the life and mission of the

Church, fostering a sense of shared responsibility and mutual support.

Moreover, both traditions emphasize the importance of personal prayer and a relationship with God. Prayer is a vital component of Christian life, fostering communication with the Divine and nurturing spiritual growth. This mutual commitment to prayer underscores the intimate connection both communities seek to cultivate with God, highlighting a common spiritual pursuit.

Our shared belief in the resurrection of the dead and the promise of eternal life further unites us. Both Roman Catholics and Protestants affirm the hope of resurrection and the assurance of everlasting life with God. This eschatological hope provides comfort and motivation, encouraging believers to persevere in their faith and live in the expectation of Christ's ultimate return.

As we move forward, it is imperative to build on these shared beliefs, allowing them to serve as bridges across our doctrinal divides. By highlighting our common ground, Roman Catholics and Protestants can engage in meaningful dialogue, fostering mutual respect and understanding. This process involves listening attentively, learning from one another, and recognizing that despite our differences, we are united in our devotion to Christ and our commitment to living out His teachings.

In conclusion, the common ground we share with Protestant communities is vast and significant. Our shared beliefs in the divinity of Christ, the Holy Trinity, the authority of Scripture, the transformative power of baptism, the necessity of grace, and the moral teachings of Jesus, among others, provide a robust foundation for dialogue and collaboration. By focusing on these areas of agreement, we pave the way for greater unity and reconciliation, strengthening the bonds of our shared Christian witness.

As we continue to navigate the path toward reconciliation, let us remember that our shared faith transcends our differences. In the words of the Apostle Paul, "There is one body and one Spirit, just as you were called to one hope when you were called; one Lord, one faith, one baptism; one God and Father of all, who is over all and through all and in all" (Ephesians 4:4-6, New International Version). This profound truth reminds us of our collective identity as members of the body of Christ, united in our mission to serve Him and spread His love.

Addressing Doctrinal Divides: Sacraments, Authority, and Scripture

In the pursuit of reconciliation between Roman Catholics and Protestant communities, a significant challenge lies in addressing the doctrinal divides—particularly those concerning sacraments, authority, and Scripture. These core elements of faith have historically been points of contention, and understanding them is essential for any meaningful dialogue.

To begin with, the sacraments serve as visible signs of invisible grace within the Roman Catholic Church. These sacraments are fundamentally rooted in the belief that they were instituted by Christ and are necessary for salvation. The Council of Trent profoundly solidified this view, articulating the necessity and efficacy of the sacraments as channels of divine grace. Protestants, however, have historically had a different perspective. Martin Luther, for example, recognized only Baptism and the Eucharist as sacraments, considering their institution by Christ in Scripture as the benchmark. This leads to a substantial divergence in theological understanding (O'Collins, 2017).

The issue of authority further complicates matters. Roman Catholicism posits that the Church, guided by the Holy Spirit, holds the Magisterium—or teaching authority—which interprets both Tradition and Scripture. This is a principle that finds its roots in the apostolic succession, thereby assuring doctrinal continuity from Christ to the present day (Congar, 1997). Conversely, Protestantism, especially in its Reformed branches, often upholds the principle of "sola scriptura," meaning Scripture alone is the ultimate authority on matters of faith and practice. This fundamental divergence impacts almost every doctrinal discussion, creating a barrier that needs careful navigation (McGrath, 2012).

Moreover, Scripture itself is a focal point for debate. Catholics hold to a canon that includes the Deuterocanonical books, which the Protestant Old Testament excludes. This difference is not merely academic but affects the entirety of scriptural exegesis and the theological insights derived from these texts. Embedded within the Protestant Reformation was a call to return to what reformers considered 'the true Gospel' as found solely within the canonical Scriptures, rejecting what they perceived as non-biblical additions (Bruce, 1988).

The Eucharist, or Holy Communion, perhaps illustrates the doctrinal chasm most vividly. The Roman Catholic Church maintains that the Eucharist is not merely symbolic but a true transubstantiation—the bread and wine become the actual Body and Blood of Christ (CCC 1376). Protestants, on the other hand, range from viewing the Eucharist as a symbolic memorial to

Martin Luther's concept of consubstantiation, where Christ is present 'in, with, and under' the elements. This theological disparity underscores deeper divergences in understanding salvation and grace.

Moving forward, it becomes crucial to emphasize commonalities without glossing over significant differences. Both traditions, for instance, agree on the paramount importance of Baptism and the Eucharist, even if their theological understandings diverge significantly. This common ground offers a basis for dialogue and potential reconciliation. Overcoming reductive caricatures of each other's beliefs and engaging with the substantive theological principles can pave the way for more fruitful discussions (Peters, 2015).

What role do Church authorities play in this reconciliation? The Roman Catholic Church's hierarchical structure, with the Pope at its apex, is often viewed with suspicion by Protestant communities, who generally favor more decentralized models of governance. The ecumenical efforts of recent papacies, from John XXIII to Francis, have demonstrated that an emphasis on collegiality and a pastoral approach to authority can foster a better mutual understanding. This doesn't negate the importance of the Petrine office but rather contextualizes it within a broader framework of service and unity (Ratzinger, 1985).

An area warranting particular focus is the hermeneutics of Scripture. The Second Vatican Council's document "Dei Verbum" highlights the necessity of tradition and the magisterium in interpreting the Word of God, whereas many Protestant traditions prioritize individual interpretation led by the Holy Spirit. This difference has led to varied doctrinal developments over the centuries (Vatican Council II, 1965). Scholars and theologians engaged in ecumenical dialogue can advance this by promoting a deeper understanding of the historical context in which these traditions took shape, thus paving the way for a more respectful and informed discourse.

The sacraments, authority, and Scripture are more than doctrinal issues; they are deeply woven into the spiritual and communal fabric of both Catholic and Protestant lives. Recognizing and respecting these differences while seeking shared ground is vital. There's no denying the complexity of reconciling centuries of doctrinal divides, but the Gospel imperative for unity remains a compelling force. Reconciliation involves a willingness to listen, an openness to learn, and a commitment to journey together in faith, seeking the truth of Christ which, ultimately, binds all believers.

Chapter 5: Dialogue with the Eastern Orthodox Church: Bridging Ancient Schisms

The dialogue between the Roman Catholic Church and the Eastern Orthodox Church is not merely an exercise in theological discourse; it is a quest for unity rooted in the very foundations of Christianity itself. This schism, dating back to the Great Schism of 1054, remains one of the most profound wounds in Christian history. Yet, despite centuries of separation, the potential for reconciliation is promising, spurred by a mutual recognition of apostolic succession and sacred traditions.

One of the most compelling aspects of this dialogue is the theological similarities that underpin both congregations. Both churches have preserved a belief in the seven sacraments, apostolic succession, and the centrality of the Eucharist. Interestingly, these shared beliefs provide a fertile ground for fostering a greater understanding. Still, ritualistic differences, which may appear superficial to the uninitiated, reveal deep-seated divergences in liturgical practices and ecclesial structures (Benedict & Schmemann, 2004).

A critical point of contention has long been the Filioque clause. The Roman Catholic insertion of "and the Son" into the Nicene Creed without an ecumenical council's approval was seen by the

Orthodox as an overreach. While some contemporary theologians argue that the Filioque is a non-essential difference, resolving this issue would be a monumental step towards unity. By engaging in frank discussions and mutual concessions, we can see this theological rift as not a barrier, but an opportunity for deeper communion (Meyendorff, 1974).

Moreover, engagement in charitable acts and social justice initiatives can serve as avenues for bridging gaps. The combined moral authority of these age-old institutions can address modern societal issues, from poverty alleviation to human rights. Indeed, working together in the public sphere serves as a powerful testament to the Christian call for unity and love.

In sum, dialogue with the Eastern Orthodox Church is not simply about hashing out theological nuances but about reuniting the mystical body of Christ. Through respectful dialogue, theological exploration, and collaborative action, the possibility of healing this ancient schism becomes not just a hopeful aspiration but a tangible reality. We are called to extend our hands across this historic divide, moving ever closer to the unity that Christ himself prayed for (John 17:21).

Theological Similarities and Ritualistic Differences

The theological landscape shared between the Roman Catholic and Eastern Orthodox churches is rich with nuances that reveal both unity and divergence. At the core, these two branches of Christianity hold a mutual foundation in the Nicene Creed, recognizing the Trinity as Father, Son, and Holy Spirit. This shared creed underscores a fundamental theological accord that has persisted even through centuries of separation. Moreover, both churches affirm the significance of sacred tradition and scripture, though their interpretive lenses and hierarchical structures offer distinct perspectives (Ware, 1997).

Beyond creedal affirmations, the doctrinal consonance extends to the sacraments, particularly the Eucharist, viewed as the actual body and blood of Christ. This Eucharistic theology signifies a profound spiritual unity, engendering the faithful's intimate connection with the Divine. Despite such consonance, ritualistic practices encircling the Eucharist exhibit conspicuous differences. The Roman Catholic Church celebrates the Eucharist with the Latin Rite liturgy, marked by the precise, codified prayers of the Roman Missal. Contrarily, the Orthodox Divine Liturgy of St. John Chrysostom or St. Basil is imbued with a sense of mystical participation, emphasizing sensory elements such as incense, icons, and chanted hymns (Taft, 1992).

Given that both traditions center the role of bishops in maintaining apostolic succession, the ecclesiological structures demonstrate a shared heritage of hierarchical oversight. Nevertheless, the Papal Primacy doctrine distinguishes the Roman Catholic understanding of governance from the collegiality-oriented Orthodox approach. The former elevates the Pope as the supreme earthly authority, the Vicar of Christ, endowed with infallibility in proclamations of faith and morals. In contrast, although the Ecumenical Patriarch of Constantinople is honored as "first among equals," he lacks the unilateral authority ascribed to the Pope, embodying more consultative rather than absolute authority (Meyendorff, 1983).

Another significant theological parallel includes the veneration of the Virgin Mary, "Theotokos," or God-bearer, in both traditions. This deeply rooted Marian devotion culminates in doctrines such as her perpetual virginity and Assumption (Roman Catholic) or Dormition (Eastern Orthodox). Yet, the Roman Catholic dogma of the Immaculate Conception, which posits Mary's freedom from original sin from the moment of her conception, remains a distinctive teaching that the Orthodox do not explicitly endorse (Pelikan, 1996).

Moving from theology to ritual, one of the more salient differences lies in baptismal practices. Both traditions administer this sacrament as the initial rite of Christian initiation involving water and the Trinitarian formula. While the Roman Church more commonly employs affusion (pouring), the Orthodox meticulously adhere to triple immersion, symbolizing Christ's three days in the tomb. Furthermore, the Orthodox Church administers confirmation (Chrismation) and Eucharist to infants immediately after baptism, contrasting with the Roman Catholic practice of Confirmation as a later, separate rite (Janes, 2001).

Lenten disciplines also manifest ritualistic variations. The Eastern Orthodox observance of Great Lent is rigorously ascetical, featuring strict fasting rules that often exclude all animal products and promote an extensive liturgical schedule. Conversely, the Roman Catholic Lenten practice, streamlined since Vatican II, involves fasting and abstinence on selected days, focusing more on personal penance and less liturgical intensity. These differentiated approaches reflect deeper spiritual idioms, where the Orthodox manner gravitates towards an immersive, communal asceticism, while the Catholic practice integrates individual penitential acts within a structured ecclesial framework (Williams, 2002).

The veneration and liturgical role of icons present another intriguing ritualistic discrepancy. Iconography in the Eastern Orthodox Church is not merely decorative but considered a theologically rich practice that offers a window to the divine, engaging the faithful in contemplative reverence. Icons are often kissed, carried in processions, and treated as pivotal elements of worship. Meanwhile, the Roman Catholic tradition, while utilizing statues and images, does not ascribe the same theological import to icons as "windows to heaven," focusing instead on the didactic and inspirational roles of these sacred images (Ouspensky & Lossky, 1982).

Confession—or the sacrament of Penance—serves as yet another area revealing ritualistic divergence while maintaining theological similarity. Both traditions uphold the necessity of confessing sins for absolution and returning to grace. In the Catholic Church, confession typically transpires within a confessional booth, involving a private dialogue between the penitent and priest. The Orthodox sacrament, however, often occurs openly in the church before an icon of Christ, with the priest standing as a witness, not as a solitary mediator. This public dimension underscores the communal nature of sin and repentance in Orthodox understanding (Theriault, 2008).

Liturgical calendars, too, express both unity and variation. Feasts such as Christmas, Easter, and Pentecost are universally celebrated, yet their calculative methods can differ. The Roman Catholic Church follows the Gregorian calendar, while the Eastern Orthodox Church adheres to the Julian calendar for many feasts, resulting in different dates for significant observances such as Easter. This calendrical divergence stems from historical, theological, and even astronomical considerations, yet it hasn't detracted from the shared centrality of these holy days (MacDonald, 2010).

In the mystical and ascetic traditions, the similarities and differences come forth strikingly. Both churches venerate monastic life as the epitome of Christian asceticism, yet the Orthodox monastic tradition, especially as seen on Mount Athos, often prioritizes hesychastic prayer—a spiritual exercise focusing on inner quietude and the repetitive invocation of the Jesus Prayer. While similar mystical traditions exist in Catholicism, such as the Carmelite or Trappist contemplative prayer, they are often more identified with "mental prayer" and the writings of mystics like St. John of the Cross and St. Teresa of Avila (Healy, 2012).

These theological and ritualistic comparisons point to the profound richness within Christian tradition. The shared doctrines fortify a common ground that makes ecumenical dialogue not only possible but fruitful. They reflect a mutual patrimony that—despite historical schisms—presents a compelling narrative of inherent unity. On the other hand, the ritualistic differences bring to light the diverse expressions of living faith, attuned to historical, cultural, and spiritual contexts that enrich the broader tapestry of Christendom.

Thus, in engaging with the Eastern Orthodox Church, Roman Catholics are invited to not only recognize these shared foundations but also to appreciate the distinctiveness that defines each tradition's approach to embodying and practicing the same faith. This delicate balance—of unity in theology and diversity in ritual—calls for a dialogue marked by both firmness in truth and openness in charity. The ultimate aim is to bridge ancient schisms with renewed understanding and respect, striving towards the unity Christ desired for his followers (John 17:21).

Resolving the Filioque: A Step Towards Unity

The dialogue between the Roman Catholic Church and the Eastern Orthodox Church has been characterized by both profound theological engagement and enduring historical tensions. Central to this conversation is the contentious issue of the Filioque clause, a single Latin term that has, for centuries, symbolized deeper ecclesiological divides. To understand the importance of resolving the Filioque dispute, we must grasp the historical development and theological implications of this term.

The Filioque, Latin for "and the Son," was incorporated into the Nicene Creed by the Western Church to clarify the double procession of the Holy Spirit — from both the Father and the Son. This addition aimed to combat Arianism, which denied the full divinity of the Son. However, the insertion was made without the consultation or consent of the Eastern Church, leading to accusations of unilateralism and theological innovation. The Eastern Orthodox Church maintains the original wording, which states that the Holy Spirit proceeds from the Father, reflecting the Cappadocian Fathers' theological articulation.

This divergence over the Filioque is more than a mere linguistic quibble; it embodies distinct theological perspectives. For the Western Church, the Filioque underscores the intimate relationship between the three Persons of the Trinity, emphasizing unity and equality. The Eastern outlook, conversely, upholds the monarchy of the Father as the sole principle (arche) of the Godhead, ensuring the Father's unique role in generating the Son and spirating the Spirit. The differing procession doctrines thus represent both theological and ecclesial identities that need harmonizing (Ware, 1995).

Attempts at resolving the Filioque have seen various degrees of success and failure throughout history. The Council of Florence (1438-1439) signaled a moment of hope for reconciliation, wherein both sides achieved a temporary agreement. The council declared that the Filioque, correctly understood, was orthodox and not heretical. Leaders from both East and West affirmed that the Spirit proceeds from the Father through the Son. However, this agreement was short-lived, as it failed to gain broader acceptance, particularly among the Eastern faithful and clergy ("Council of Florence", 2004).

In recent decades, dialogues initiated by the Second Vatican Council (1962-1965) have reopened discussions on the Filioque. Vatican II's emphasis on ecumenism and the desire for unity among all Christians instigated fresh conversations aimed at overcoming historical grievances and miscommunications. The council's decrees highlighted the need to respect and understand the doctrinal positions of the Eastern Orthodox

Church, recognizing the profound theological richness and apostolic continuity present within it (Abbott, 1966).

Consequently, the Joint International Commission for Theological Dialogue between the Roman Catholic Church and the Orthodox Church has devoted significant efforts to this matter. Contemporary dialogues have moved towards a consenseral pedagogy where mutual respect and a desire for true understanding reign supreme. Documents like the "Balamand Declaration" and the "Ravenna Document" have elucidated shared perspectives while acknowledging remaining differences. A promising development is the growing consensus that the original Nicene-Constantinopolitan Creed should be the common text for all Christians, recognizing the Filioque as a legitimate, albeit optional, theological expression within the Western tradition.

In these dialogues, the Catholic Church has demonstrated a willingness to make concessions for the sake of unity. Some theologians even suggest that the Filioque clause could be omitted during ecumenical liturgies with the Orthodox, thereby respecting their tradition without compromising doctrinal integrity. This approach fosters an environment of reciprocity and goodwill, which is paramount for genuine unity.

From a philosophical perspective, resolving the Filioque controversy is essential to transcending historical particularities and achieving the universal call for Christian unity. The metaphysical underpinnings of Trinitarian theology underscore the importance of relationality within the Godhead, reflecting divine love, which should serve as a model for human interactions and ecclesial relations. The relational ontology in Trinitarian thought offers a paradigm where diversity within the unity of the Church can be celebrated rather than suppressed (Zizioulas, 1985).

Moreover, the resolution of the Filioque issue serves to counteract theological provincialism, encouraging both churches to engage in a more expansive understanding of the divine mystery. As theologians like Yves Congar suggest, the path to unity often requires a "reconversion" to the core tenets of faith, demanding both humility and openness to the Spirit's guidance (Congar, 1970). This reconversion must be simultaneously intellectual, spiritual, and practical — engaging believers at every level of the Church.

The stakes of resolving the Filioque are not purely academic or historical; they bear substantial ramifications for the Church's witness in the modern world. In an era marked by secularism and fragmentation, the visible unity of Christians can serve as a powerful testament to the reconciling and transcendent power of the Gospel. Unity among the Roman Catholic and Eastern Orthodox Churches can act as a catalyst for broader Christian cooperation and testimony, embodying Christ's prayer "that they may all be one" (John 17:21).

In sum, addressing the Filioque clause's theological and historical dimensions requires a multifaceted approach, characterized by scholarly rigor, ecclesial sensitivity, and spiritual integrity. It is a step towards not only reconciling two ancient Christian traditions but also offering a unified Christian witness to a fractured world. By fostering dialogue rooted in the spirit of Vatican II and inspired by the rich theological legacies of both the Eastern and Western Churches, this reconciliation can become a significant milestone on the path to Christian unity.

Let us echo the words of the Council of Constantinople in 553: "The Holy Spirit, who proceeds from the Father and the Son, indivisibly along with the same substance, one God" — a theological articulation that, while complex, reflects the earnest pursuit of truth and unity that our shared faith demands. As we move forward, may the Holy Spirit guide us to transcend our historical boundaries and embody the unity that reflects the very nature of God.

In this way, resolving the Filioque dispute isn't just about doctrinal precision but about participating in the divine mission of reconciliation and unity. It invites both the Roman Catholic and Eastern Orthodox Churches to revisit, rearticulate, and reconcile their theological narratives, fostering a future where the fullness of Christian truth can be proclaimed with one voice.

Chapter 6: Encounters with Islam: Understanding and Respect

As we delve into our exploration of interfaith dialogues, we reach one of the most significant relationships in the modern religious landscape: the interaction between Roman Catholicism and Islam. The necessity for understanding and respect in these encounters cannot be overstated. A nuanced appreciation of each other's foundational beliefs and practices is essential for fostering mutual respect and dispelling misconceptions.

To begin with, Catholicism and Islam share deep Abrahamic roots. Both traditions revere figures such as Abraham, Moses, and Mary, albeit within different theological frameworks. This shared heritage presents a remarkable opportunity for engagement but also underscores profound doctrinal divergences. It is vital for Catholics to understand Islam not merely as a monolithic entity but as a diverse faith encompassing various interpretations and traditions (Esposito, 2017).

The Second Vatican Council, through documents like "Nostra Aetate," laid the groundwork for a respectful dialogue with Muslims. This pivotal text recognizes the moral and spiritual values found within Islam and calls for mutual understanding and collaboration for social justice and peace (Vatican Council II,

1965). This ecumenical spirit invites Catholics to engage with Muslims in a spirit of fraternity while upholding the truth of Christ's unique salvific role.

Although the commonalities are significant, it is imperative for Roman Catholics to remain cognizant of the theological chasms that lie between the two faiths. The concept of the Trinity, the divinity of Jesus, and the sacramental life of the Church are fundamentally at odds with Islamic doctrines. Engaging with these doctrinal differences respectfully and thoughtfully is necessary for authentic dialogue (Lumen Gentium, 1964).

One of the most pressing challenges in Catholic-Muslim dialogue is the mutually pervasive secularism and atheism in contemporary societies. Both religious communities face the erosion of spiritual values and an increase in secular ideologies that often marginalize religious beliefs. This common struggle offers an unprecedented opportunity for Catholics and Muslims to collaborate in defending the sacred against a 'dictatorship of relativism' (Ratzinger, 2005).

Moreover, Catholics are called to emulate Christ's compassion and respect when interacting with Muslims. This principle of love and respect does not imply relinquishing our profound theological convictions but encourages a form of evangelization that is both respectful and honest. In these encounters, it is essential to prioritize a relational and dialogic approach, emphasizing shared values while not shying away from discussing differences (Benedict XVI, 2006).

In light of the diverse tapestry of Islamic beliefs and practices, developing a holistic and nuanced understanding is vital. This posture facilitates not only informed dialogues but also diminishes the space for radicalism and ignorance. Encouraging academic and grassroots interfaith initiatives can aid in these efforts, creating avenues for genuine relationships and cooperative action (Mitchell, 2019).

In conclusion, encounters with Islam necessitate a combination of theological clarity and relational empathy. Through Vatican II's vision, Catholics are provided with a robust framework to engage Muslims respectfully and thoughtfully. By recognizing our shared Abrahamic heritage and collaborating against secular challenges, Catholics and Muslims can build a foundation for mutual respect. This respect paves the way for a witness to the spiritual truths of Roman Catholicism, inviting Muslims and all people into a deeper understanding of God's salvific love.

Shared Abrahamitic Roots: Commonality and Contention

It is no secret that Islam, Christianity, and Judaism all trace their roots to the patriarch Abraham. To understand the commonalities and contentions emerging from this shared heritage, it is crucial to delve into the theological and historical intricacies that lie beneath the surface. The purpose of this exploration is twofold: to foster an appreciation for shared sacred history and to elucidate the points of divergence that have historically caused friction between Islam and Christianity.

Abraham, known as Ibrahim in Islam, is revered across these faiths as a paragon of monotheistic belief. In the Christian tradition, Abraham is celebrated for his unwavering faith, as exemplified by his willingness to sacrifice his son Isaac at God's command (Genesis 22:1-19). Similarly, in Islamic tradition, Abraham's faith is highlighted, albeit with a focus on his readiness to sacrifice Ishmael instead (Quran 37:100-112). The variations in these narratives underscore the theological contentions but also point to Abraham's central role in both traditions as an archetype of devout submission to God.

One of the primary commonalities among these Abrahamic faiths is the concept of monotheism. Islam vigorously upholds the oneness of God (tawhid), much like Christianity professes the doctrine of the Trinity—an understanding of one God in three persons: Father, Son, and Holy Spirit. While both faiths worship one God, the Christian understanding of the Trinity and the Islamic tawhid are often points of contention, invoking varied theological understandings (Nasr, 2009).

Ethical monotheism, another shared aspect, implies not just the belief in one God, but also a set of moral imperatives derived from that belief. For example, both faiths advocate for acts of charity, justice, and piety. In the Quran, zakat, or almsgiving, is fundamental, as is charity in the Christian tradition, often emphasized through the teachings of Jesus. Prophet Muhammad and Jesus both exemplify ethical leadership, urging followers to live righteous lives, although the theological motivations behind such ethics may differ (Brown, 2003).

Scripturally, both Islam and Christianity hold their sacred texts in the highest regard. The Quran in Islam is considered the literal word of God as revealed to Muhammad. In Christianity, while the Bible's divine inspiration is recognized, it is also understood through the lens of Sacred Tradition and Holy Scripture, as articulated by the magisterium of the Church. This difference in scriptural interpretation and authority can complicate interfaith dialogue. Nevertheless, recognizing the Holy Scriptures as divine revelations links these faiths in their mutual quest for understanding God's will.

Yet, the figure of Jesus Christ presents significant theological divides. To Christians, Jesus is the Son of God, the second person of the Holy Trinity, fully divine and fully human. The Incarnation, Crucifixion, and Resurrection of Jesus are central tenets of Christian faith. On the other hand, Islam views Jesus (Isa) as one of the greatest prophets, born of the virgin Mary but not divine or crucified. These contrasting views on the nature and role of Jesus elevate a pivotal point of theological contention (Partridge, 2005).

Another crucial aspect for discussion involves salvation. Christianity teaches that salvation is through Jesus Christ, a core belief stemming from Christ's sacrificial death and Resurrection. This stands in contrast with Islamic soteriology, which posits that salvation is achieved through submission to Allah and adherence to the Five Pillars of Islam. The different soteriological frameworks provide a salient point for interfaith discussions aimed at understanding each other's spiritual economies.

Furthermore, life's final destinies—heaven and hell—are integral, yet distinct concepts within these traditions. For Catholics, heaven is eternal communion with God made possible by Jesus' redemptive sacrifice, and purgatory is a transitional state for souls. In Islam, heaven (Jannah) is seen as the eternal reward for those who live righteously according to Allah's will, while hell (Jahannam) is for those who reject the divine guidance. The eschatological visions enrich the theological texture of each religion while underlining the differing pathways to eternal destiny.

Cultural and historical interactions between Christians and Muslims further augment these theological contentions. The Crusades, Reconquista, and various colonial enterprises have left scars and foster misconceptions that require historical scrutiny and reconciliation. Despite these historical tensions, there were periods of intellectual and spiritual exchanges, such as the translation movements in medieval Spain, where Islamic and Christian scholars engaged in meaningful dialogue, contributing significantly to scientific and philosophical advancements (Esposito, 1988).

In contemporary times, the spirit of Vatican II has encouraged a renewed effort towards dialogue and understanding between these faiths. The declaration "Nostra Aetate" acknowledges the shared Abrahamic heritage and calls for mutual respect and cooperation. This declaration has been instrumental in opening doors for collaborative efforts in addressing modern secularism and atheism, thereby facilitating a joint witness to the relevance of faith in a pluralistic world.

In conclusion, the shared Abrahamic roots of Islam and Christianity offer a rich tapestry of commonality and contention. Understanding these nuances goes beyond theological gymnastics; it serves as a foundation for mutual respect and cooperation, necessary for peaceful coexistence. As Roman Catholics, recognizing these shared roots compels us to engage in dialogue with empathy and a genuine desire for truth, always bearing in mind the Church's mission to be a light to the nations.

- - -

The Challenge of Secularism and Atheism in Dialogue

The intersection of secularism, atheism, and Islamic theology presents a unique set of challenges for those engaged in interfaith dialogue, particularly for the Roman Catholic Church. This complexity stems from different foundational worldviews: where secularists and atheists often operate from a perspective grounded in rationalism and empirical science, Islamic theology is deeply rooted in the Qur'anic revelation and long-standing traditions. Bridging these divergent paths requires not only a firm understanding of Catholic doctrine but also an appreciation for the nuanced beliefs held by secularists, atheists, and Muslims. This multi-faceted dialogue enables a deeper appreciation of Catholic theology's robustness when juxtaposed against other belief systems.

One significant obstacle in this engagement is the oft-proclaimed incompatibility of faith and reason, especially emphasized by secular and atheistic perspectives. Atheists typically argue that belief in God and religious doctrines lack empirical evidence and rational justification (Dawkins, 2006). On the contrary, Islam emphasizes the harmony between faith and reason, seen as complementary rather than antagonistic. The Catholic Church, since the time of St. Augustine and St. Thomas Aquinas, has also embraced a synthesis of faith and reason. Vatican II reaffirmed this approach, encouraging Catholics to "recognize, preserve, and promote the good things, spiritual and moral, as well as the socio-cultural values found among" other religious traditions (Vatican II, 1965).

For dialogue to be fruitful, Catholics must recognize the genuine concerns of atheists and secularists regarding religious truth claims. This requires a balanced approach that respects the empirical rigor valued by secularists while also affirming the metaphysical truths of the faith. The Catholic intellectual tradition has long held that truth is one, whether discovered through reason or revelation. This principle allows Catholics to engage with secular thinkers on common grounds of rationality and shared ethical values while gradually introducing the transcendent truths revealed through Christ.

Islam presents a different yet equally complex dialogue partner. Islamic theology shares certain Abrahamic roots with Christianity but diverges sharply on key doctrinal points, such as the understanding of Jesus Christ and the concept of original sin. When engaging with Muslims, it's crucial for Catholics to clarify these doctrinal differences respectfully and thoughtfully. At the same time, secularism and atheism often pose a challenge to Islamic societies, which are generally less secularized than their Western counterparts. This dual challenge requires a nuanced approach that navigates the particular socio-cultural contexts of Muslim communities.

Addressing atheism and secularism in the context of Islamic societies often involves engaging with intellectual currents that critique religious authority and question traditional values. This scrutiny is sometimes viewed as a threat to the coherence and stability of Muslim societies, which, similar to Catholicism, place a significant emphasis on community and moral order. The Catholic approach, then, must be one that seeks common ground in ethical principles while addressing secular critiques with theological and philosophical rigor.

The Catholic Church's perspective on human dignity and moral law offers a rich vein of commonality with both secular humanists and devout Muslims. While secularists may reject a theistic foundation for morals, many still affirm universal human rights and innate dignity. Similarly, Islamic teachings uphold the sanctity and dignity of human life as created by God. Thus, interfaith dialogue can prioritize these shared values as a springboard for deeper discussions about divine revelation and moral truth.

Another dimension to consider is the role of Western colonialism and its lasting impact on the relationships between religious traditions and secularism. Both Catholic and Islamic societies had to contend with the secular ideologies introduced during and after colonial times, which sometimes resulted in a defensive stance against secular modernity. A meaningful dialogue must address these historical wounds and pave the way for a candid exchange of ideas, facilitating mutual understanding and reconciliation.

The Church must also confront the challenge of moral relativism that often accompanies secularism. Secular societies frequently espouse a relativistic view of ethics and truth, which stands in stark contrast to the moral absolutism found in Catholic teaching. This provides an opportunity for Catholics to present the transcendent moral law, illuminated by natural law theory and divine revelation, which offers a coherent basis for universal ethics. Such a dialogue demands not only theological acumen but also a profound philosophical grounding to articulate why some moral truths are indeed universal and immutable.

Moreover, the pedagogical aspect cannot be ignored. Engaging secular and atheistic views requires a pedagogical strategy that promotes religious literacy and critical thinking among both Catholics and their dialogue partners. The Church, guided by the principles of Vatican II, must endeavor to educate its faithful on the contributions of secular and Islamic thought to human understanding, thereby fostering a more informed and empathetic dialogue. Simultaneously, it must elucidate the profound depth and coherence of Catholic theology, highlighting its capacity to address the existential questions that secularism and atheism attempt to grapple with.

In fostering these dialogues, the Church draws upon its rich intellectual tradition, which has historically engaged with the broader currents of thought. The writings of Church Fathers and Scholastic theologians provide invaluable resources for addressing the challenges posed by secular and atheistic arguments. Their works demonstrate that faith seeking understanding is not a static pursuit but a dynamic engagement with the fullness of truth, revealed in Christ and explored through reason.

Encounters with secularism and atheism also challenge the Church to witness to the transformative power of faith in Christ. This testimony is particularly potent when articulated through lives of holiness, charity, and intellectual honesty. The witness of contemporary Catholic thinkers who engage constructively with secular and atheistic ideas encourages a model of dialogue grounded in mutual respect and a shared quest for truth.

In conclusion, the dialogue between Roman Catholicism, secularism, and atheism, especially in the context of Islamic theology, is a multifaceted endeavor requiring humility, intellectual rigor, and a commitment to truth. By recognizing the legitimate concerns and values of secularists and atheists,

Catholics can present a compelling case for the faith that resonates with the deepest longings of the human spirit. Simultaneously, engaging with Islam on doctrinal differences and shared ethical values fosters a mutual respect that enriches both traditions. Through respectful dialogue and intellectual engagement, the Catholic Church can bear witness to the enduring truth and spiritual superiority of its teachings, as inspired by Vatican II and grounded in the timeless truths of faith and reason.

Chapter 7: The Jewish-Catholic Relationship Post-Vatican II

The Second Vatican Council (Vatican II) marked a transformative period in the relations between the Catholic Church and the Jewish community. Historically fraught with tension and misunderstanding, the Council initiated a new era of reconciliation and mutual respect. The declaration "Nostra Aetate," promulgated by Pope Paul VI in 1965, was a pivotal document that reshaped the Catholic stance towards Judaism. It unequivocally repudiated anti-Semitism and acknowledged the enduring covenant between God and the Jewish people (Flannery, 1996).

Anti-Semitism, an insidious blight that marred Christian-Jewish relations for centuries, found a formidable adversary in Vatican II. The Council disavowed the age-old charge of deicide traditionally levied against Jews and called upon Catholics to foster a spirit of brotherhood. This theological pivot is more than a mere doctrinal adjustment; it encapsulates a profound moral awakening. Addressing the dark history of anti-Semitism within the Church requires ongoing reflection and actionable steps towards healing old wounds (Boys, 2000).

Vatican II also brought to light the importance of shared sacred texts. Both Catholics and Jews revere the Hebrew Scriptures, providing a common ground for dialogue and collaboration.

Recognizing these shared scriptures does more than just create a theologically rich milieu for dialogue; it also underscores the depth of our spiritual kinship. Despite significant doctrinal divergences, such as the Catholic belief in the New Testament, this mutual reverence promotes a collective appreciation of divine revelation (Kasper, 2015).

The post-Vatican II era has seen numerous interfaith initiatives aimed at fostering understanding between Catholics and Jews. Educational programs, joint religious services, and theological dialogues have become frequent. These activities, undergirded by the Church's revised teachings, seek to break down barriers and create lasting bonds of friendship.

In summary, the Jewish-Catholic relationship post-Vatican II represents a promising evolution from hostility to hope, from suspicion to solidarity. The efforts made post-Vatican II are testament to a shared aspiration for truth, anchored in the divine love that we both seek to manifest in this world.

Anti-Semitism and the Church: Healing Old Wounds

The Jewish-Catholic relationship has been fraught with tension, misunderstanding, and at its worst, outright hostility for centuries. However, the Second Vatican Council (Vatican II) marked a significant turning point in the Church's posture towards Judaism. The Council's magnum opus, Nostra Aetate, brought about a paradigm shift intended to heal the festering wounds of anti-Semitism, realigning the Church's position toward a more inclusive and respectful dialogue. This section delves into this reformation and the consequential steps towards mending the historical rift.

Understanding the depth of anti-Semitism in Church history requires a look back at various prejudices perpetuated through theological teachings and societal attitudes. For centuries, Jews were labeled as "Christ-killers" and were subjected to various forms of persecution, including expulsions, forced conversions, and pogroms. This tragic history is not merely an unfortunate series of episodes but reflects a fundamental misunderstanding and misrepresentation of Jewish people within Christian theology.

The declaration of Nostra Aetate during Vatican II addressed these historical wrongs by emphasizing the shared heritage of Christians and Jews. It explicitly repudiated the notion of collective Jewish guilt for the crucifixion of Jesus Christ. Nostra Aetate asserts, "True, the Jewish authorities and those who followed their lead pressed for the death of Christ (cf. John 19:6); still, what happened in his passion cannot be charged against all the Jews, without distinction, then alive, nor against the Jews of today" (Nostra Aetate, 1965). This profound statement marked a significant pivot in Church doctrine, shining a light on the need for repentance and reform.

One cannot overstate the importance of this acknowledgment, yet Nostra Aetate was more than just a condemnation of past prejudices; it was an invitation to dialogue and mutual respect. The document underscores the spiritual bond between Christianity and Judaism, acknowledging that "the beginnings of [the Church's] faith and her election are to be found in the patriarchs, Moses and the prophets" (Nostra Aetate, 1965). By recognizing the shared scriptural and theological foundations, the Church opened avenues for collaborative scholarship and interreligious dialogue.

This effort to heal wounds did not end with words on a document. Pope John Paul II, in 1986, significantly strengthened these efforts by being the first pope to visit a synagogue, symbolizing a path toward reconciliation. His declaration, "You are our dearly beloved brothers, and, in a certain way, it could be said that you are our elder brothers" (John Paul II, 1986), resonated deeply within both communities. Such gestures, paired with theological reform, showcase an earnest commitment to moving beyond historical grievances.

Efforts to combat anti-Semitism have continued into the 21st century. Pope Benedict XVI and Pope Francis have both made substantial contributions to this ongoing dialogue. Pope Benedict's theological work emphasized the roots of Christianity in Judaism, while Pope Francis has maintained a close friendship with Jewish communities, often participating in joint initiatives aimed at promoting peace and mutual understanding. Francis declared, "Due to our common roots, a Christian cannot be anti-Semitic!" (Pope Francis, 2015). These proclamations and actions have fortified the bridge between the two faiths.

However, acknowledging past mistakes and issuing official documents is just the beginning. Theologically rooted prejudices require persistent education and dialogue. The Church has made strides in this area by promoting a deeper understanding of Judaism within its seminaries and educational institutions. Textbooks and curricula have been revised to reflect a more accurate portrayal of Jewish beliefs and traditions, fostering an atmosphere of mutual respect and scholarly exchange.

Moreover, these efforts have extended beyond formal education into community engagements and interfaith collaborations.

Parishes around the world have initiated local dialogue groups, fostering personal relationships that aim to dispel lingering myths and build mutual understanding. These grassroots efforts have proved invaluable in applying the principles of Nostra Aetate in everyday life.

Importantly, this journey towards reconciliation aligns with the broader theological vision of the Church. Recognizing the shared monotheistic tradition and ethical frameworks of both Judaism and Christianity encourages a cooperative pursuit of social justice, peace, and human dignity. This collaboration underscores a unified moral vision that transcends doctrinal differences, promoting the common good.

In striving to mend these old wounds, the Church embodies the theological virtues of faith, hope, and charity. It's an enduring testament to the transformative power of repentance and reconciliation. While much progress has been made, the work continues, as ingrained prejudices and misunderstandings are not easily uprooted. The commitment to this path, however, remains steadfast, echoing through continued dialogue, education, and mutual respect.

In conclusion, the Catholic Church's efforts since Vatican II to heal the wounds of anti-Semitism represent a profound shift toward humility, repentance, and collaborative dialogue. By recognizing the shared heritage and mutual respect between Catholics and Jews, the Church sets a hopeful precedent for interfaith relations worldwide. This journey, deeply rooted in theological and philosophical principles, continues to evolve, reminding us of the ever-urgent need to confront prejudice and promote unity in a fragmented world.

Celebrating Shared Scripture, Recognizing Divergence

The Jewish-Catholic relationship, particularly post-Vatican II, represents a rich tapestry woven with both shared threads and distinct patterns. At the heart of this relationship lies a profound engagement with shared scripture. The Hebrew Bible, or the Old Testament as Christians refer to it, forms a foundational text for both Jews and Roman Catholics, linking the two faiths inextricably through narrative, law, and prophecy. Yet, the same scriptures also highlight vital differences, serving as points of theological and interpretative divergence.

For centuries, Catholicism has revered the Hebrew Scriptures, seeing in them the foreshadowing and prophecy of Christ. Vatican II's "Nostra Aetate" marked a pivotal moment in encouraging Catholics to recognize the Jewish roots of their faith, urging a renewed respect and understanding of Jewish traditions and interpretations of shared texts (Second Vatican Council, 1965). This shift was not merely an act of ecumenism but a theological declaration that honored the continuity and sanctity of the Jewish covenant with God.

One cannot ignore the role that shared scripture has played in fostering a sense of kinship between Jews and Catholics. The narratives of creation, the patriarchs, the exodus, and the commandments are not merely historical accounts but living memories that shape the moral and spiritual ethos of both communities. For Catholics, these stories find fulfillment in the New Testament, creating a continuum that Jews do not recognize in the same theological sense. The challenge and beauty of post-Vatican II dialogue lie in celebrating this shared heritage while respecting the profound differences in interpretation and meaning (Flannery, 1998).

Indeed, celebrating shared scripture has served as a unifying force in Catholic-Jewish relations. Catholic scholars have increasingly turned to Jewish exegeses to gain deeper insights into the Old Testament. An example is the medieval Jewish commentator Rashi, whose work has provided valuable context for Catholic biblical scholars. Such cross-pollination enriches understanding and fosters an atmosphere of mutual respect (Johnson & Anderson, 2004). It is an intellectual endeavor that goes beyond theological debate, opening doors to interfaith cooperation and deeper appreciation of each other's traditions.

However, divergence begins to manifest prominently when the discussion shifts to the New Testament. For Catholics, the New Testament is the fulfillment of the promises made in the Old Testament. Jesus Christ is seen as the long-awaited Messiah, a belief that is central to Catholic doctrine but is not shared by Jews. This fundamental difference marks a clear theological boundary that, while often approached with respect, remains a point of division between the two faiths. It is this very divergence that invites rich dialogue and necessitates a careful, respectful approach to interfaith discussions.

Understanding these divergences requires a philosophical lens as well as a theological one. Catholicism, in its essence, views the Old Testament through a Christological framework. Typology, for example, is a method where Catholics interpret Old Testament figures and events as prefigurations of Christ. Consider the story of Isaac's near-sacrifice by Abraham, often paralleled with Christ's crucifixion. For Jews, Isaac's story stands independently within its own covenantal framework, not as a mere prelude to another narrative (O'Collins, 2012).

In these areas of divergence, there lies a philosophical opportunity to embrace both mystery and humility. As G.K. Chesterton once suggested, the presence of mystery in religious practice and belief is not a hindrance but rather an essential component that invites deeper adoration and contemplation. For interfaith dialogue, this means recognizing that while we may follow different paths, the search for divine truth is a journey that can be shared with companionship and respect.

Recognition of divergence is as essential as the celebration of shared scripture in fostering a resilient and respectful relationship. Theologically, both Jews and Catholics need to acknowledge their unique identities and distinctive understandings of the divine narrative. This mutual recognition can act as a foundation for genuine dialogue, providing a platform for discussing broader issues that impact both communities, such as secularism, ethical dilemmas, and social justice. By having a clear understanding of both shared perspectives and differences, meaningful progress can be made in these areas.

Moreover, the embracing of scriptural commonalities and differences serves a broader ecumenical purpose, one that aligns with Vatican II's call for Catholics to engage in constructive dialogue with all religions. By setting an example of respectful and enriching dialogue with Jewish communities, Catholics pave the way for similar interactions with other faith traditions, contributing to a global culture of understanding and peace. This larger mission is integral to the very essence of Catholic teachings post-Vatican II, reflecting the Church's universal call to love and unity (Gonzalez, 2014).

Initiatives like the study of Jewish texts in Catholic seminaries, joint scriptural studies, and interfaith services underscore the concrete steps taken to celebrate shared scripture. These practices nurture a shared sense of sacredness while acknowledging theological boundaries. It promotes an environment where both Jews and Catholics can worship, contemplate, and learn together, enriching each other's spiritual journeys.

Celebrating the shared scripture between Jews and Catholics, while recognizing the theological divergences, offers a profound message: unity in diversity. It is an expression of how deep-rooted traditions and divergent theologies can coexist in a symphony of dialogue, mutual learning, and respect. Through this approach, the Catholic Church not only honors its commitment to its own faith but also to the broader human quest for understanding the divine.

Ultimately, Vatican II's vision for Jewish-Catholic relations was not about erasing differences but about embracing them within a framework of shared humanity and divine worship. It encourages both faith communities to see scripture not as battlegrounds for theological supremacy but as sacred texts that bring them closer to God in their own unique ways. This is not just an academic endeavor but a spiritual and philosophical journey, one that invites Catholics and Jews alike to enter into a relationship characterized by genuine respect, mutual enrichment, and transcendent love.

Chapter 8: Engaging with Eastern Religions: Buddhism, Hinduism, and Beyond

In our increasingly interconnected world, engaging with Eastern religions such as Buddhism and Hinduism is not just an academic exercise; it is a necessity for those committed to the missionary spirit of the Roman Catholic Church. Understanding these traditions in their depth while witnessing to the transcendent truth of Catholicism is a delicate but indispensable task. The Catholic Church, which values the diverse expressions of human religiosity, encourages genuine dialogue for the ultimate goal of proclaiming Christ to all nations.

Buddhism, with its teachings on suffering, impermanence, and enlightenment, presents both a challenge and an opportunity for Catholic evangelization. Interestingly, the Four Noble Truths of Buddhism carry a semblance to the Christian understanding of the human condition and the need for salvation. Both traditions grapple with suffering, albeit from different perspectives. While Buddhism views desire as the root of all suffering, Christianity identifies sin as the fundamental cause. Here lies a potent entry point for dialogue: Catholic theology, enriched by the Paschal Mystery, offers a more holistic solution through the redemptive act of Christ's suffering, death, and resurrection.

Hinduism, with its rich pantheon of deities and its intricate philosophical systems, might seem far removed from monotheistic Catholicism. Nevertheless, it provides avenues for meaningful engagement, particularly through the concept of the divine. Hinduism's understanding of Brahman, the ultimate reality, can act as a bridge to discuss God's nature from a Catholic standpoint. St. Paul's sermon at the Areopagus (Acts 17:22-31) serves as an apt model here: he recognized the Athenians' religiosity and used it as a stepping stone to preach the Gospel. A similar approach can be adopted in dialogues with adherents of Hinduism, highlighting that their spiritual yearnings find true fulfillment in the triune God made known through Jesus Christ.

Moreover, Hinduism's cyclical view of time and reincarnation contrasts sharply with the Christian linear understanding of history, emphasizing a definitive beginning and an ultimate end—Alpha and Omega. The resurrection of the body and eternal life is the Christian hope, which provides clarity and purpose beyond the cycles of samsara. For many Hindus, this perspective can be not just compelling but liberating.

In engaging with these religions, one must emphasize respect without compromising the truth. Vatican II's document "Nostra Aetate" underscores the importance of recognizing the "goodness and truth" present in other religions while acknowledging that full revelation and means of salvation subsist in the Catholic Church (Vatican Council II, 1965). This balance between respect and witness is crucial.

Finally, the mystical traditions within Buddhism and Hinduism often resonate deeply with the Catholic mystical tradition. Figures like St. John of the Cross and Teresa of Avila, who delved into the depths of Christian mysticism, can provide intriguing parallels and contrasts for meaningful dialogue. Catholicism's profound sacramentality and understanding of prayer enrich these conversations, presenting a full and embodied path to encountering the divine.

The mission remains to witness to the fullness of truth as revealed in Jesus Christ while acknowledging and engaging with the profound mysteries that these rich religious traditions present. Through this respectful and thoughtful dialogue, we hope to draw others closer to the ultimate reality, who is God Himself, lovingly revealed in the person of Jesus Christ, and present in His Church.

Respecting Mystical Traditions While Witnessing to Catholic Truth

Engaging with the mystical traditions of Eastern religions presents a nuanced yet profound opportunity to witness to the Catholic truth. Both Buddhism and Hinduism exhibit rich spiritual traditions that emphasize mystical experience and personal enlightenment. However, in presenting Catholicism's truths, it is essential to do so with a profound sense of respect and understanding of these mystical traditions. The goal is not merely to contrast but to find areas of genuine spiritual connection that can pave the way for a deeper dialogue and mutual enrichment.

First and foremost, it is imperative to recognize the common ground in the search for transcendence. Both Catholicism and the mystical practices of Eastern religions seek ultimate union with the divine or a higher state of consciousness. Despite differing theologies and metaphysical constructs, this shared yearning underscores humanity's universal quest for meaning and spiritual fulfillment. This commonality offers a platform for constructive dialogue, rather than adversarial confrontation.

The Dalai Lama, in his teachings, often speaks of compassion and the cessation of suffering. These are principles that resonate deeply with Catholic social and spiritual teachings. Catholicism's deep commitment to acts of charity and the alleviation of human suffering can find an echo in Buddhist practices of compassion (Dalai Lama, 2005). While the doctrinal foundations differ—Catholicism rooted in the love of Christ and Buddhism in the Noble Eightfold Path—the practical applications often converge in meaningful ways.

Moreover, Hinduism's concept of 'Brahman,' the ultimate reality, has parallels with the Catholic understanding of God's omnipresence and omnipotence. Although Catholics understand God in Trinitarian terms, the mystical yearning in Hinduism for merging with Brahman can be seen as a metaphor for the Christian's quest for unity with God. This sense of union is vividly described in the mystical works of St. John of the Cross and St. Teresa of Avila. These saints describe their spiritual journeys toward an intimate relationship with God, often in terms that feel profoundly relatable to those engaged in Hindu mystical practices.

However, while embracing these similarities, Catholics must also witness to the truth as revealed by Jesus Christ. The revelation of the Trinity, the Incarnation, and the salvific act of Christ's crucifixion and resurrection are non-negotiable tenets of Catholic faith. In situations of interfaith dialogue, it is essential to assert these truths clearly yet compassionately. Scholars such as Fr. Raimon Panikkar have advocated for a dialogical approach that deeply respects the other yet maintains the integrity of Catholic doctrine (Panikkar, 1981).

This process involves not only talking but also listening. It involves studying the sacred texts, rituals, and spiritual practices of other religions with an open heart. Vatican II's document, Nostra Aetate, encourages this respectful engagement, stating: "The Catholic Church rejects nothing that is true and holy in these religions. She regards with sincere reverence those ways of conduct and of life, those precepts and teachings which...often reflect a ray of that Truth which enlightens all men" (Vatican II, 1965).

In engaging with Buddhists and Hindus, it is particularly fruitful to focus on the mystical and contemplative dimensions of our faith. Practices such as Christian meditation and the contemplative prayer highlighted by figures like Thomas Merton and Fr. Thomas Keating resemble certain Eastern practices in their methods of achieving deep spiritual awareness. Merton, in his dialogue with Eastern monks, often found that the Catholic contemplative path resonates profoundly with Buddhist meditative practices (Merton, 1968).

Christians must remember that true evangelization is an act of love. As such, it should inspire us to appreciate the profound spiritual wisdom found in other traditions even as we bear witness to the unique and transformative message of the Gospel. A constructive example of this approach can be seen in the works of the Federation of Asian Bishops' Conferences, which fosters engagement with Asian religions to promote mutual understanding and respect.

Additionally, efforts in religious dialogue should not solely aim for intellectual agreement but also foster genuine spiritual encounters. This dynamic exchange can lead to what Pope John Paul II called a "dialogue of life," where people of different faiths live and work together in harmony, discovering God's presence in their shared experiences (John Paul II, 1990).

Engaging with Eastern religions through the lens of respect and witness is thus a delicate balancing act. It requires that Catholics stay faithful to the core tenets of their faith while being open to the richness of other spiritual traditions. This approach can enrich the spiritual lives of all involved, fostering a world where religious diversity becomes a fountain of blessing rather than a source of division.

In conclusion, the Catholic Church encourages its faithful to witness to the truths of Christianity while genuinely respecting and understanding the mystical traditions of other religions. Through respectful dialogue and mutual enrichment, Catholics can engage deeply with the spiritual depth of Buddhism,

Hinduism, and other Eastern traditions, revealing the universal call to divine truth and unity under the auspices of Christ's eternal love.

Chapter 9: Gregarious Mission: Evangelization in a Respectful Manner

Evangelization, in its essence, is the sharing of the Good News—in this case, the eternal truth of Roman Catholicism. It demands a delicate balance of zeal and respect, compassion and conviction. The term "gregarious mission" underscores our communal responsibility to share our faith graciously, without coercion or condescension. The goal isn't to impose belief but to invite understanding, to illuminate the profound joys and truths of the Roman Catholic faith.

Historically, the Church's approach to evangelization has been manifold, rooted in both proclamation and witness. The Second Vatican Council revitalized this mission, emphasizing dialogue and mutual respect among different faith traditions (Dulles, 2002). This transformation beckons us to not only preach the gospel but to live it through authentic relationships and ethical interactions. We are called to be beacons of hope, charity, and truth in a world that sorely needs these virtues.

The contemporary Catholic must be well-versed in both their own faith and the beliefs of others. This knowledge forms the foundation for respectful and effective evangelization. Ignorance, on the other hand, often breeds misunderstandings and conflicts. Therefore, a deep understanding of Catholic teachings, coupled with a genuine interest in other faith traditions, is indispensable. It's about creating bridges, not barriers, about fostering dialogue rather than disputation.

Endowed with this dual knowledge, the faithful can engage in meaningful conversations, offering the Catholic perspective with humility and clarity. Respect for the listener is paramount. Arrogance or insensitivity can erase the gains of even the most theologically sound arguments. Remember, the ultimate aim is conversion of hearts, a process that must be nurtured gently and patiently (Rahner, 1966).

Importantly, evangelization today cannot ignore the pluralistic context in which it occurs. We live in an interconnected world where the digital realm offers unprecedented opportunities for spreading the Gospel. However, these opportunities must be navigated with the same respect and dignity as face-to-face interactions (Gormally, 2011). The advancements in communication should augment our mission, not distort it.

To conclude, the gregarious mission of evangelization in a respectful manner engages the faithful in a dual practice of living and proclaiming the Gospel. By combining zeal with respect, knowledge with humility, and tradition with innovation, we can carry forward the Church's sacred mission in a fragmented world. This approach invites curiosity, nurtures dialogue, and, most importantly, respects the dignity of every person encountered.

The Roman Catholic Church as a Beacon of Hope in a Fragmented World

In a world increasingly characterized by fragmentation and dissonance, the Roman Catholic Church stands as a beacon of hope and unity. This is not merely a matter of historical inertia or institutional longevity; rather, it is rooted in the timeless truths and divine mission that the Church embodies. Through its unwavering commitment to the teachings of Christ, the Church offers a cohesive narrative that addresses the existential questions and moral dilemmas of our time.

The Church's mission of evangelization, grounded in respect and love, seeks to fulfill Christ's Great Commission in a manner that recognizes the dignity of every human being. Rooted in the theological concept of "Missio Dei" (the mission of God), the Church perceives itself not as an isolated entity but as a participant in God's ongoing redemptive work in the world (Bosch, 1991). Consequently, the Church's outreach strategies are imbued with a deliberate respect for the cultural and religious contexts into which she enters, all while steadfastly proclaiming the salvific truth of the Gospel.

Evangelization in a respectful manner necessitates a two-fold approach: proclamation and dialogue. The Catholic Church, especially post-Vatican II, has intricately balanced these elements. On one hand, it proclaims the Gospel as an invitation to conversion and new life in Christ. On the other, it engages in genuine dialogue with other faith traditions, recognizing that seeds of truth reside outside its visible boundaries. This dual approach allows the Church to act as a unifying force, offering a holistic vision of human dignity and salvation.

The notion of the Church as a beacon of hope is not merely a theological assertion but has practical implications. One need only to look at the Church's numerous social justice initiatives, charitable organizations, and educational institutions that serve millions around the globe. Through organizations like Caritas Internationalis and the Pontifical Council for Justice and Peace, the Church actively works to alleviate poverty, address systemic inequality, and promote human rights, thereby exemplifying the love of Christ in action (Caritas Internationalis, 2020).

Historically, the Catholic Church has also been a custodian of educational and scientific advancements. From the medieval universities of Europe to contemporary Catholic schools and universities worldwide, the Church has consistently promoted the pursuit of truth, integrating faith and reason. This rich intellectual tradition continues to provide ethical and philosophical guidance, especially in a fragmented world where moral relativism often reigns supreme (Hollis, 2009).

One cannot overlook the symbolic and real hope offered by Catholic liturgy and sacraments. These rites are not mere rituals but are imbued with profound theological meaning. The Eucharist, often referred to as the "source and summit of the Christian life," offers spiritual nourishment and unity, encapsulating the entire mystery of salvation in Christ (Second Vatican Council, 1965). Through the sacraments, the faithful are continually drawn into deeper communion with God and with each other, reinforcing the Church's role as a community of hope.

In discussions about ecumenical and interfaith dialogue, it is imperative to note the Church's unique position. Raised in an intellectual and spiritual tradition that combines faith with reason, the Church is well-equipped to engage with diverse worldviews. Its contributions to interfaith dialogue are not driven by a desire to dilute religious differences but rather to build mutual respect and understanding, fostering a global community that mirrors the inclusive call of the Gospel (Dulles, 2001).

The Church's understanding of human suffering and its redemptive value is also a significant pillar of hope. In a fragmented world marked by suffering and despair, the Catholic doctrine of "Redemptive Suffering" offers solace and meaning. It teaches that suffering, when united with Christ's own passion and sacrifice, has a purifying and sanctifying effect, both for the individual and the world. This view transforms suffering from a meaningless ordeal into a profound participation in the divine mystery, thereby providing hope even in the darkest of times (John Paul II, 1984).

Furthermore, the Church's ethical teachings, encapsulated in documents like the *Catechism of the Catholic Church* and various Papal encyclicals, offer clear moral guidance in an age of ethical ambiguity. The Church's stance on issues such as the sanctity of life, the definition of marriage, and social justice is informed by a well-developed moral theology that seeks the common good and human flourishing. These teachings not only serve to unify the faithful but also act as a moral compass for wider society.

Culturally, the Roman Catholic Church has made significant contributions to art, music, and literature, which continue to inspire and uplift humanity. From the Sistine Chapel to the works of Bach and Beethoven, Catholic-inspired art and culture have been a source of beauty and contemplation. These cultural contributions are not mere aesthetic achievements but manifestations of the divine, pointing towards a higher reality and offering a respite from the fragmentation of worldly concerns (O'Connell, 2014).

Lastly, the Church's universal nature—as *catholica*, or "universal"—affirms its mission to be a source of unity across diverse cultures, languages, and nations. The very structure of the Church, with the Pope as a symbol of unity and the bishops in communion with him, demonstrates an ecclesial model that resists fragmentation. This unity is not uniformity but a harmonious diversity that reflects the Trinitarian nature of God Himself.

In sum, the Roman Catholic Church serves as a beacon of hope in a fragmented world through its divine mission of evangelization carried out in a respectful manner. By preaching the Gospel and engaging in genuine dialogue, through its social justice initiatives and intellectual contributions, and by offering ethical guidance and cultural enrichment, the Church illuminates pathways to unity and peace. Grounded in its rich sacramental life and undergirded by a theology of redemptive suffering, the Church stands firm as a sign of hope, embodying the compelling call to transform a fragmented world into a more unified and loving reflection of the Kingdom of God.

As we continue to navigate the complexities of the modern world, the Church's unchanging mission serves as both a spiritual anchor and a guiding light, drawing all people towards the eternal truth and universal call to salvation.

The Eternal Truth and the Universal Call to Salvation

As we reach the conclusion of this work, we must contemplate the essence of the Roman Catholic faith—an essence that transcends temporal boundaries and cultural divides. This eternal truth forms the bedrock of a universal call to salvation, a call that echoes through the corridors of history and reverberates in the hearts of those seeking spiritual fulfillment. In a world marked by pluralism and diverse religious traditions, the Catholic Church stands as a singular beacon, inviting all humanity into a communion that is both mystical and transformative.

Latin phrases like "Extra Ecclesiam nulla salus" ("Outside the Church, there is no salvation") have historically underscored this universal call. While its interpretation has evolved, the essence remains rooted in the belief that the fullness of salvific truth resides within the Catholic Church. Vatican II, a watershed moment in modern Catholic thought, heralded a more inclusive understanding of this doctrine, emphasizing dialogue and mutual respect among different faith traditions. Yet, this does not dilute the Church's claim to possess the fullness of divine revelation. Instead, it challenges us to recognize this truth in a manner that is both inviting and encompassing (O'Malley, 2010).

It is essential to understand that this universal call is not a call to mere conversion, but to a deeper, transformative relationship with Christ, as mediated through His Church. The sacraments, Sacred Scripture, and Sacred Tradition serve as indispensable instruments in this divine economy of salvation. To engage with other religions while maintaining this truth is a delicate balancing act, requiring both intellectual humility and theological conviction. It is through this delicate balance that the Roman Catholic Church can maintain its doctrinal integrity while extending the hand of fellowship to those outside its fold (Rahner & Vorgrimler, 1965).

Engaging with Protestant communities, Eastern Orthodox Christians, Muslims, Jews, Buddhists, Hindus, and adherents of other faiths, the Catholic Church's mission has been one of respectful invitation rather than forceful proselytization. This approach is grounded in the acknowledgment of shared values and common ground but always pointing to the unique and unparalleled revelations afforded by the Catholic tradition. By recognizing and revering the seeds of truth present in other faiths, Catholics bear witness to the ultimate truth encapsulated in the Church's teachings. Even as we acknowledge the worth of other traditions, we must assert, with confidence and charity, the Roman Catholic Church's role as the ark of salvation (Flannery, 1996).

Salvation history, as unveiled through Catholic doctrine, reaches its zenith in the ultimate reconciliation of humanity with God. This reconciliation is not just an esoteric spiritual aspiration but a lived reality, manifesting through the Church's sacraments and moral teachings. These sacraments, especially the Eucharist, serve as the loci of Divine-human encounter, bridging the finite with the infinite. As such, the Church is not merely an institution but the living Body of Christ, continuously sanctifying and guiding the faithful towards their final destiny—union with God.

The Roman Catholic Church also recognizes the unique challenges posed by secularism and atheism. In confronting these ideologies, the Church employs reasoned argumentation and philosophical inquiry, addressing the questions and doubts of modernity with the wisdom accumulated over centuries. This engagement is not an exercise in intellectual domination but an invitation to explore the profound mysteries of existence through the lens of faith and reason. Thus, the Church fulfills its role as both a custodian of eternal truth and a guide for souls navigating the complexities of contemporary life (Fisher, 1993).

In this universal call to salvation, the process of the Rite of Christian Initiation of Adults (RCIA) plays a pivotal role in integrating individuals from diverse backgrounds into the Catholic fold. This process is not merely a series of catechetical instructions but a profound journey of conversion and spiritual growth. As aspirants gradually immerse themselves in the sacramental life of the Church, they experience a transformation that is both personal and communal. This journey into the depths of Catholicism is emblematic of the Church's broader mission to lead all souls towards their ultimate end—eternal communion with the Triune God.

To echo the words of the Second Vatican Council, the Church "exists to reveal and communicate the love of the invisible God" (Lumen Gentium, 1964). This revelation is not bound by cultural or temporal constraints but is an everlasting invitation to partake in the divine life. As we stand on the threshold of a new era marked by increased interfaith dialogue and mutual understanding, the Catholic Church's call remains steadfast. In recognizing and embracing this call, we participate in a grand divine plan that encompasses all creation.

In conclusion, the eternal truth of the Roman Catholic Church and its universal call to salvation constitute a profound mystery, one that demands both intellectual assent and heartfelt acceptance. As we engage with believers of different faiths, the charge remains clear—to illuminate the path to Christ, ever mindful of our sacred duty to witness to the fullness of truth. Through the sacramental life, theological richness, and moral teachings of the Church, we are continually summoned to participate in the salvific mission that began with Christ and finds its ultimate fulfillment in the eschaton. In this eternal truth and universal call, lies not just the hope for individual salvation but the redemption of the entire cosmos.

Appendix A: Appendix

The intricate process of Rite of Christian Initiation of Adults (RCIA) serves as a vital mechanism for integrating believers from diverse religious backgrounds into the Roman Catholic faith. This appendix elucidates its phases, requirements, and theological significance. Embracing fully the spirit of Vatican II and the Church's long tradition of evangelization, RCIA aims to foster spiritual growth and unity among new converts.

RCIA is divided into several distinct stages, each marked by specific rites and rituals. These phases include the Period of Evangelization and Precatechumenate, the Catechumenate, the Period of Purification and Enlightenment, and the Mystagogy. Each stage is designed to guide the individual progressively deeper into the truths and responsibilities of the Catholic faith. These periods are not merely procedural but are impregnated with spiritual depth and profound theological import.

First, the Period of Evangelization and Precatechumenate is an informal yet fundamental stage where prospective converts, known as inquirers, explore the basics of the faith. During this time, they engage in discussions, partake in prayer meetings, and immerse themselves in the community. This period is instrumental in laying the foundation of genuine interest and initial conversion.

The Catechumenate marks a formal commitment to join the Church. Catechumens undergo extensive catechetical instruction, delving into Sacred Scripture, the Creed, the Ten Commandments, the Sacraments, and the Lord's Prayer. Theologically, this period is an existential journey, nurturing a robust understanding of divine revelation and the ecclesial community (Dallen, 1986).

The subsequent Period of Purification and Enlightenment usually coincides with Lent. It serves as a time of intense spiritual preparation, involving deeper prayer, examination of conscience, and penance. The scrutinies, exorcisms, and presentations of the Creed and the Lord's Prayer during this period are pivotal liturgical acts, fostering spiritual purification and enlightenment.

The final stage, Mystagogy, follows the reception of the Sacraments of Initiation—Baptism, Confirmation, and Eucharist—at the Easter Vigil. Mystagogy is not merely a conclusion but a commencement into a lifelong journey of faith. During this time, the neophytes reflect on their sacramental experiences, integrate fully into the parish community, and continue catechesis to deepen their understanding of the mysteries they have embraced.

The theological underpinnings of RCIA are grounded in the commitment to individual spiritual growth and the ecclesial nature of the Church. The initiation process embodies the Church's mission to welcome new members, fostering a collective identity rooted in shared beliefs and communal practices (Dulles, 1992).

Liturgically, RCIA's structure encapsulates the Church's sacramental theology, emphasizing the transformative grace conferred through the sacraments. The rites are not mere formalities but profound encounters with the divine, underscoring the Church's mediating role between God and humanity.

Furthermore, RCIA is a practical manifestation of the Church's universal call to holiness. Through catechesis and sacramental participation, converts are equipped to live out their faith authentically and steadfastly, contributing to the Church's mission of evangelization and sanctification of the world.

In essence, RCIA is more than a series of religious instructions; it is a holistic, transformative process that cultivates a deeper communion with God and the Church. By intertwining catechesis, liturgy, and community life, RCIA fosters an integrated faith experience, nurturing individuals to live out the Catholic faith in its fullness.

The Process of Rite of Christian Initiation of Adults (RCIA) Explained

The Rite of Christian Initiation of Adults (RCIA) is a profound and intricate process designed to initiate adults into the Roman Catholic Church. This multifaceted journey serves as a testament to the richness and depth of Catholic spiritual and communal life. The RCIA is not merely a ceremony but a transformative journey that encompasses various stages, leading the catechumens through a deep conversion and a closer relationship with God.

This process serves as both a spiritual and intellectual formation, designed meticulously to guide adults who express a desire to convert to Catholicism. The RCIA is deeply rooted in the liturgical and ecclesial traditions of the Church, aligning with the theological and pastoral directives elucidated in Vatican II. The adaptation of the RCIA program, stemming from early Christian practices, is also reflective of the Church's commitment to clarity and authenticity in the faith journey of new members (Flannery, 1996).

The initial stage of RCIA is known as the "Period of Evangelization and Precatechumenate." This is an informal phase where individuals, known as "inquirers," explore the basic tenets of the Christian faith and discern their calling. It's a time marked by personal reflection and preliminary dialogue with the Church community, embodying the Church's well-known approach of gradual immersion into its sacramental and spiritual life. This period is characterized by its open and welcoming nature, allowing inquirers to seek answers to fundamental questions about faith, God, and the Church.

The transition from the Precatechumenate to the next stage, the "Period of the Catechumenate," is marked by the Rite of Acceptance into the Order of Catechumens. This rite is a significant milestone, symbolizing the inquirer's formal admission into the journey toward full communion with the Catholic Church. The Church community acknowledges their intent and offers support through prayers and the guidance of sponsors. During this period, catechumens engage in deeper doctrinal and spiritual formation, typically involving catechetical instruction, participation in liturgical celebrations, and personal prayer (DeGidio, 2007).

The Catechumenate establishes a rigorous process that dives into the truths of the faith, the understanding of Sacred Scripture, and the fundamentals of Catholic doctrine. This phase continues until the catechumens display sufficient readiness to proceed to the next stage. Generally, this period lasts for several months, aligning with the liturgical cycle and emphasizing the gradual nature of conversion.

The third stage is the "Period of Purification and Enlightenment," often coinciding with the liturgical season of Lent. This period is marked by the Rite of Election, celebrated on the first Sunday of Lent, where catechumens, now called "the elect," publicly declare their readiness to enter fully into the sacramental life of the Church. The bishop, as the chief shepherd of the diocese, acknowledges their readiness in this ceremonious rite. For the elect, this period is a time of intense spiritual preparation, involving profound introspection, penitential rites, and the Scrutinies—rituals conducted to uncover and heal what is weak and to strengthen what is strong (Turner, 2000).

The Scrutinies, celebrated on the third, fourth, and fifth Sundays of Lent, play a pivotal role during this phase. These rites are meant to purify the minds and hearts of the elect, instilling them with a deeper conversion and an intensified resolve to follow Christ. The Church also presents the Creed and the Lord's Prayer to the elect during this period, signifying their forthcoming reception into the faith and their responsibility in living it out. This intense period of spiritual soul-searching prepares the elect for the sacraments of initiation that they will receive at the Easter Vigil.

The culmination of the RCIA journey occurs during the Easter Vigil, the greatest and most solemn liturgy of the liturgical year.

During the Easter Vigil, the elect receive the Sacraments of Initiation: Baptism, Confirmation, and Eucharist. These sacraments are conferred within the same celebration, highlighting their interconnectedness and the fullness of their initiation into the Body of Christ. The initiation of the neophytes, as they are now called post-initiation, represents their full entrance into the life of Christ and the Church.

The final stage of the RCIA is the "Period of Postbaptismal Catechesis or Mystagogy." This period, extending throughout the Easter season and beyond, offers the neophytes an opportunity to delve deeper into the mysteries they have encountered through the sacraments. Mystagogy emphasizes the lived experience of the sacraments, allowing the neophytes to grow in their understanding and appreciation of their new life in Christ. It's a time for them to become more deeply integrated into the Church community and to continue exploring and strengthening their faith through ongoing catechesis and community support.

The RCIA process is a testament to the Church's commitment to welcoming new members with sincerity and depth. It isn't just a period of preparation but a holistic journey that encompasses intellectual formation, spiritual growth, and communal integration. Through RCIA, the Church provides a structured yet profoundly personal process that allows individuals to encounter the fullness of the Catholic faith and initiate a lifelong journey with God at its center.

Embedded in the RCIA is the Church's recognition of the unique journey of each individual. The process is adaptable, as pastoral needs and individual circumstances may require adjustments in its implementation. Despite its structured format, the RCIA remains a dynamic and responsive process, emphasizing the personal vocation and spiritual readiness of each catechumen. The flexibility of RCIA exemplifies the Church's pastoral wisdom and deep care, aligning with its mission to evangelize and nurture faith (Rite of Christian Initiation of Adults, 1987).

In sum, the RCIA is more than a program; it is an embodiment of the Church's mission to bring souls into communion with Christ, develop robust spiritual lives, and foster vibrant participation in the communal and sacramental life of the Church. It synthesizes theological understanding and pastoral care, reflecting the Church's rich tradition and its continual renewal and adaptation. Through this sacred process, the Church not only welcomes new members but also renews itself, invigorating its mission of evangelization and its witness to the world.

Glossary of Terms

Ad Limina Visit: A traditional visit that bishops make to the Vatican to report on the status of their dioceses and meet with the Pope for advice and directives.

Apologetics: The theological practice of defending and explaining the Christian faith, often by addressing objections and providing reasoned arguments.

Bishop: A high-ranking clergy member in the Roman Catholic Church who oversees a diocese, controls religious ordinances, and conducts confirmation and ordination.

Canon Law: The body of laws and regulations developed or adopted by ecclesiastical authority for governing the Catholic Church (Codex Iuris Canonici).

Communion of Saints: The spiritual solidarity that binds together the faithful on earth, the souls in purgatory, and the saints in heaven in a single Church.

Consistory: A formal meeting of the Sacred College of Cardinals convened by the Pope to discuss important Church affairs, including the creation of new cardinals.

Deacon: An ordained minister who serves the Church in various capacities, assisting bishops and priests in preaching, preparing the altar, and administering baptisms.

Ecclesiology: The theological study of the Church's nature, structure, and function, focusing on its role as a community and the means of salvation.

Ecumenism: The initiatives and activities aimed at promoting unity among different Christian denominations and the broader reconciliation between all Christians.

Encyclical: A formal letter or teaching document from the Pope, usually addressed to the bishops of the Church, that discusses issues of doctrine, morals, or discipline.

Episcopal Conference: A national or regional assembly of bishops who coordinate their administrative and pastoral activities to address common concerns within their jurisdictions.

Ex Cathedra: Literally meaning "from the chair," this term refers to pronouncements made by the Pope that are considered infallible when defining doctrine concerning faith or morals.

Filioque: A Latin term meaning "and the Son," added to the Nicene Creed in the Western Church to express that the Holy

Spirit proceeds from both the Father and the Son. This phrase has been a point of contention between the Eastern Orthodox and Roman Catholic Churches.

Grace: The free and unmerited favor of God, given primarily through the sacraments, which enables humans to attain salvation and live a holy life.

Holy See: The central governing body of the Roman Catholic Church, consisting of the Pope and the Roman Curia, which governs the Vatican City State and is a sovereign entity in international law.

Inculturation: The process by which the Church adapts its teachings, liturgies, and practices to different cultures without compromising its core doctrines.

Indulgence: A remission of temporal punishment for sins, granted by the Church and stemming from the treasury of the merits of Christ and the saints.

Laity: The members of the Church who are not part of the clergy but are responsible for living out their baptismal mission to evangelize and serve within secular society.

Liturgical Calendar: The schedule of feasts, seasons, and observances within the Church year, guiding the rhythm of worship and remembrance of significant events in salvation history.

Magi: Also known as the Wise Men, these were the learned individuals from the East who visited the infant Jesus, signifying the recognition of Christ by the Gentiles.

Magisterium: The Church's teaching authority, exercised by the Pope and the bishops in communion, which guides the faithful in understanding and living out Christian doctrine.

Marian Doctrine: Teachings and beliefs related to Mary, the Mother of Jesus, including the Immaculate Conception, perpetual virginity, and the Assumption.

Monasticism: A way of life in which individuals dedicate themselves to asceticism, prayer, and communal living, often in a monastery, to grow closer to God.

Mystagogy: The final period of the Christian initiation process (RCIA) where new Catholics reflect on their sacramental experiences and deepen their understanding of the faith.

Ordinary Time: The liturgical period outside of the major liturgical seasons of Advent, Christmas, Lent, and Easter, marked by regular Sunday worship and the growth in ordinary life and discipleship.

Papal Bull: An official papal letter or document, authenticated by a leaden seal (bulla), that issues decrees on various doctrinal or administrative matters.

Real Presence: The belief that Jesus Christ is truly present in the Eucharist, body, blood, soul, and divinity, under the appearances of bread and wine.

Religious Orders: Communities of men or women who live according to a specific set of religious rules and vows, such as poverty, chastity, and obedience, to follow Christ more closely.

Rite of Christian Initiation of Adults (RCIA): The process by which adults are gradually introduced to the Roman Catholic Church's beliefs and practices, ultimately receiving the sacraments of initiation—Baptism, Confirmation, and the Eucharist.

Rosary: A devotional prayer that meditates on significant events in the lives of Jesus and Mary, composed of a series of repeated prayers, including the "Hail Mary" and the "Our Father."

Sacrament: An outward sign instituted by Christ to give grace, encompassing rites like Baptism, Eucharist, Confirmation, Reconciliation, Anointing of the Sick, Matrimony, and Holy Orders.

Transubstantiation: The doctrine that, during the consecration in the Mass, the substance of bread and wine is transformed into the substance of the body and blood of Christ, although the appearances of bread and wine remain.

Universal Call to Holiness: The teaching that all members of the Church, regardless of their state in life, are called to be saints and live a life of holiness and virtue.

Vatican II: The Second Vatican Council, an ecumenical council held between 1962 and 1965, which aimed to renew the Church's approach to the modern world, including increased interfaith dialogue and liturgical reforms.

Vicar of Christ: A title for the Pope, denoting his role as

Select Bibliography

A comprehensive understanding of the Roman Catholic Church's doctrines, dogmas, and its multifaceted role in the global religious landscape necessitates an extensive and well-curated bibliography. Scholars, theologians, and students can delve deeper into the rich theological, historical, and philosophical foundations underpinning Roman Catholicism through an array of seminal works.

To elucidate the intricate relationship between Sacred Tradition and Sacred Scripture, one might begin with Henri de Lubac's pivotal texts. De Lubac, a leading figure in the ressourcement movement that influenced Vatican II, provides an expansive view of how tradition and divine revelation interweave within the Catholic faith (De Lubac, 2007). His work is fundamental in understanding the Church's self-conception as the guardian of divine truth.

Any serious study of the Second Vatican Council requires engagement with "The Documents of Vatican II," edited by Walter M. Abbott. This anthology offers the original documents along with commentaries that reflect the theological and pastoral shifts initiated by the council (Abbott, 1966). It's indispensable for appreciating Vatican II's innovative approaches to ecumenism and interfaith dialogue, affecting all aspects of modern Catholic thought.

For those exploring the challenges and merits of interfaith dialogue, Karl Rahner's "Theological Investigations" is a valuable resource. Rahner delves into themes pertinent to the Church's encounter with other religions, such as anonymous Christianity and the possibility of salvation outside the institutional Church (Rahner, 1961). This collection of essays broadens one's perspective on inclusive yet theologically grounded approaches to interreligious engagement.

To further understand the historical outreach of Catholicism, Robert Louis Wilken's "The First Thousand Years: A Global History of Christianity" offers a panoramic view of the Church's early endeavors to establish connections beyond its immediate geographic and cultural confines (Wilken, 2012). This historical study shines a light on the formative interactions between the Catholic Church and other world religions, crucial for grasping contemporary ecumenical challenges.

In addressing the complex reconciliation process with Protestant communities, Jaroslav Pelikan's "The Riddle of Roman Catholicism" examines both common theological ground and enduring doctrinal conflicts (Pelikan, 1959). Pelikan's scholarship, rich with historical and theological insights, provides a balanced foundation for understanding the roots and possibilities of Protestant-Catholic dialogue.

The Eastern Orthodox Church, with its deeply rooted traditions and theological depth, is another critical area of study. Timothy Ware's "The Orthodox Church" serves as an indispensable guide to the theological similarities and ritualistic differences that have both united and divided Eastern Orthodoxy and Roman Catholicism over centuries (Ware, 1993). It's essential for anyone seeking to bridge the ancient schisms between these two apostolic traditions.

Regarding Catholic-Muslim relations, John L. Esposito's "Islam: The Straight Path" offers a clear and accessible introduction to Islamic beliefs and practices, laying a foundation for respectful dialogue and understanding (Esposito, 2011). Esposito's nuanced approach is invaluable for Catholics looking to engage constructively with the Muslim community.

Post-Vatican II Jewish-Catholic relations have seen substantial developments, detailed effectively in "Dabru Emet: Jews and Christians in Dialogue" by David Novak. Novak's work presents a series of theological dialogues and documents highlighting the ongoing process of reconciliation and mutual understanding between these two faith traditions (Novak, 2000). This book is pivotal for anyone studying the Church's efforts to redress historical grievances and build future cooperation.

For encounters with Eastern religions such as Buddhism and Hinduism, "Christianity and World Religions" by Hans Küng provides a thorough comparative study. Küng's exploration of these mystical traditions and their commonalities with Christian spirituality enhances our appreciation of religious pluralism while affirming Catholic truth (Küng, 1986). This text helps delineate the respectful yet assertive approach the Church advocates in interreligious dialogue.

Finally, Michael Novak's "The Catholic Ethic and the Spirit of Capitalism" examines the socio-economic dimensions of Catholic teaching, making it a useful addition to anyone interested in understanding the Church's role in the modern world. Novak's reflections on how Catholic values intersect with contemporary issues present an applicable perspective on the broader mission of the Church today (Novak, 1993).

These works, among many others, form a robust foundation for engaging with the core themes presented in this book. By diving deep into these resources, scholars and students alike can attain a more comprehensive understanding of the Catholic Church's theological, historical, and ecumenical positions, paving the way for meaningful dialogue and spiritual growth.

References

1. Fisher, E. J., 1993. Faith Without Prejudice: Rebuilding Christian Attitudes Toward Judaism. Crossroad Publishing Company.

2. Flannery, A., 1996. Vatican Council II: The Conciliar and Post-conciliar Documents. Liturgical Press.

3. O'Malley, J. W., 2010. What Happened at Vatican II. Harvard University Press.

4. Rahner, K., & Vorgrimler, H., 1965. Theological Dictionary. Herder and Herder.

5. Abbot, W. M. (1966). *The Documents of Vatican II*. America Press.

6. Abbott, W. M. (Ed.). (1966). The Documents of Vatican II. America Press.

7. Abbott, W. M. (Ed.). (1966). The Documents of Vatican II. Crossroad Publishing Company.

8. Benedict, P. & Schmemann, A. (2004). Eastern Orthodox Christianity: A Western Perspective. Crestwood, NY: St. Vladimir's Seminary Press.

9.   Boys, M. C. (2000). Jewish-Christian Dialogue: One Woman's Experience. Paulist Press.

10. Brown, J. A. (2003). *The Canonical Quran: Distinguishing Textual Elements within Islam's Holy Book*. Oxford University Press.

11. Bruce, F. F. (1988). The Canon of Scripture. InterVarsity Press.

12. CCC. (1994). Catechism of the Catholic Church. Libreria Editrice Vaticana.

13. Caritas Internationalis. (2020). Annual Report.

14. Catechism of the Catholic Church. (1994). Libreria Editrice Vaticana.

15. Catechism of the Catholic Church. (1994). Vatican: Libreria Editrice Vaticana.

16. Catechism of the Catholic Church. (1994). Vatican: Libreria Editrice Vaticana.

17. Catechism of the Catholic Church. (1997). Retrieved from https://www.vatican.va/archive/ENG0015/_INDEX.HTM

18. Congar, Y. (1997). The Meaning of Tradition. Ignatius Press.

19. Congregation for Sacred Liturgy and the Sacraments. (1963). Sacrosanctum Concilium. In The Documents of Vatican II. Vatican Press.

20. Congregation for the Doctrine of the Faith. (1965). Dei Verbum. In The Documents of Vatican II. Vatican Press.

21. Congregation for the Doctrine of the Faith. (2000). Declaration Dominus Iesus. Retrieved from https://www.vatican.va/roman_curia/congregatio ns/cfaith/documents/rc_con_cfaith_doc_2000080 6_dominus-iesus_en.html

22. Council of Florence. (2004). In E. Fahlbusch & G. W. Bromiley (Eds.), The Encyclopedia of Christianity (Vol. 2, pp. 491-492). Brill.

23. Dalai Lama. (2005). *The universe in a single atom: The convergence of science and spirituality*. Harmony Books.

24. Dawkins, R. (2006). The God Delusion. Houghton Mifflin Harcourt.

25. De Lubac, H. (2007). Medieval Exegesis: The Four Senses of Scripture. Eerdmans Publishing.

26. DeGidio, S. (2007). Rite of Christian Initiation of Adults: A Pastoral Liturgical Commentary. Liguori, MO: Liguori Publications.

27. Duffy, E. (1997). Saints and Sinners: A History of the Popes. Yale University Press.

28. Dulles, A. (1992). The Church. New York: Image Books.

29. Dulles, A. (2001). Theology of the Church. University of Notre Dame Press.

30. Dulles, A. (2002). Models of the Church. New York: Image Books.

31. Esposito, J. L. (1988). *Islam: The Straight Path*. Oxford University Press.

32. Esposito, J. L. (2011). Islam: The Straight Path. Oxford University Press.

33. Esposito, J. L. (2017). Islam: The Straight Path. Oxford University Press.

34. Fenton, J. C. (1958). The Concept of Salvation Outside the Church in Selected Theological Writings of Saint Thomas Aquinas. The Catholic University of America Press.

35. Flannery, A. (1996). *Vatican Council II: The Conciliar and Post-Conciliar Documents*. Costello Publishing Company.

36. Flannery, A. (1996). Vatican Council II: Constitutions, Decrees, Declarations. Costello Publishing Company.

37. Flannery, A. (1996). Vatican Council II: The Conciliar and Post Conciliar Documents. Liturgical Press.

38. Flannery, A. (1996). Vatican Council II: The Conciliar and Postconciliar Documents. Collegeville, MN: Liturgical Press.

39. Flannery, A. (1996). Vatican Council II: The Conciliar and Post Conciliar Documents. Costello Publishing Company.

40. Flannery, A. (1998). *Vatican Council II: The
     conciliar and post conciliar documents*. Liturgical
     Press.

41. Gonzalez, J. L. (2014). *The Story of Christianity:
     Volume 2: The Reformation to the Present Day*.
     HarperOne.

42. Gormally, L. (2011). Ethical issues in modern
     communication. Journal of Catholic Ethics and
     Theology, 12(1), 34-47.

43. Healy, N. M. (2012). Thomas Aquinas: Theologian
     of the Christian Life. Ashgate Publishing.

44. John Paul II. (1984). Salvifici Doloris: On the
     Christian Meaning of Human Suffering.

45. John Paul II. (1986). Address at the Synagogue of
     Rome.

46. John Paul II. (1990). *Redemptoris Missio* (On the
     permanent validity of the Church's missionary
     mandate).

47. Johnson, P., & Anderson, R. (2004). *Teaming Up: Shared Leadership in Schools*. Association for Supervision and Curriculum Development.

48. Jørgensen, J. (2008). Witness to Hope: The Biography of Pope John Paul II. Harper Collins.

49. Kasper, W. (2015). The Catholic Church. Nature, Reality and Mission. Bloomsbury T&T Clark.

50. Keener, C. (2020). Biblical Imagery of the Church as Bride of Christ. Journal of Theological Studies, 67(3), 254-278.

51. Küng, H. (1986). Christianity and World Religions. Doubleday.

52. Martos, J. (2001). Doors to the Sacred: A Historical Introduction to Sacraments in the Catholic Church. Liguori/Triumph.

53. McBrien, R. P. (2006). The Church: The Evolution of Catholicism. HarperOne.

54. McGrath, A. E. (2012). Reformation Thought: An Introduction. Wiley-Blackwell.

55. Merton, T. (1968). *Mystics and Zen Masters*.
Farrar, Straus, and Giroux.

56. Meyendorff, J. (1974). Byzantine Theology:
Historical Trends and Doctrinal Themes. New
York, NY: Fordham University Press.

57. Mitchell, J. (2019). Interfaith Dialogue: A Guide for
Muslims. Amana Publications.

58. Murray, J. C. (1966). *The Declaration on Religious
Freedom of Vatican Council II*. Sheed and Ward.

59. Murray, J. C. (1966). Dignitatis Humanae: In
Religious Liberty: Catholic Struggles with
Pluralism. Westminster John Knox Press.

60. Nasr, S. H. (2009). *The Garden of Truth: The
Vision and Promise of Sufism, Islam's Mystical
Tradition*. HarperOne.

61. New International Version. (n.d.). Ephesians 4:4-6.
Bible Gateway. Retrieved from
https://www.biblegateway.com/passage/?search
=Ephesians+4%3A4-6&version=NIV

62. Newman, J. H. (1845). Essay on the Development of Christian Doctrine. J. Toovey.

63. Nostra Aetate. (1965). Declaration on the Relation of the Church to Non-Christian Religions.

64. Novak, D. (2000). Dabru Emet: Jews and Christians in Dialogue. Oxford University Press.

65. Novak, M. (1993). The Catholic Ethic and the Spirit of Capitalism. Free Press.

66. O'Collins, G. (2017). The Second Vatican Council on Other Religions. Oxford University Press.

67. O'Connell, M. (2014). The Desire of the Everlasting Hills: The World Before and After Jesus. Image.

68. Oesterreicher, J. M. (1971). The New Encounter Between Christians and Jews. Philosophical Library.

69. O'Collins, G. (2012). *Jesus: A Portrait*. Orbis Books.

70. Panikkar, R. (1981). *The unknown Christ of Hinduism* (revised ed.). Orbis Books.

71. Paul VI. (1964). Lumen Gentium. Vatican Council II: The Basic Sixteen Documents.

72. Pelikan, J. (1959). The Riddle of Roman Catholicism. Abingdon Press.

73. Pelikan, J. (1984). The Vindication of Tradition. Yale University Press.

74. Peters, E. (2015). Sacraments. In J. P. Beal (Ed.), New Commentary on the Code of Canon Law. Paulist Press.

75. Pope Francis. (2015). Address to the International Jewish Committee on Interreligious Consultations.

76. Rahner, K. (1961). Theological Investigations. Helicon Press.

77. Rahner, K. (1966). Theological investigations. London: Darton, Longman & Todd.

78. Ratzinger, J. (1985). Church, Ecumenism, and Politics: New Essays in Ecclesiology. Crossroad Publishing Company.

79. Ratzinger, J. (2005). *Principles of Catholic Theology: Building Stones for a Fundamental Theology*. Ignatius Press.

80. Ratzinger, J. (2005). Truth and Tolerance: Christian Belief and World Religions. Ignatius Press.

81. Ratzinger, J. (2005). Church, Ecumenism, and Politics: New Endeavors in Ecclesiology. Ignatius Press.

82. Ratzinger, J. (2008). Jesus of Nazareth: From the Baptism in the Jordan to the Transfiguration. Doubleday.

83. Schillebeeckx, E. (1985). Church: The Human Story of God. New York: Crossroad.

84. Second Vatican Council. (1965). *Nostra Aetate: Declaration on the Relation of the Church to Non-Christian Religions*. Vatican Polyglot Press.

85. Second Vatican Council. (1965). Lumen Gentium: Dogmatic Constitution on the Church.

86. Turner, P. (2000). The Catechumenate Answer Book. Chicago, IL: Liturgy Training Publications.

87. Vatican Council II. (1963). Sacrosanctum Concilium. Retrieved from https://www.vatican.va/archive/hist_councils/ii_vatican_council/documents/vat-ii_const_19631204_sacrosanctum-concilium_en.html

88. Vatican Council II. (1964). Lumen Gentium. In A. Flannery (Ed.), Vatican Council II: The Conciliar and Post Conciliar Documents (pp. 15-74). Liturgical Press.

89. Vatican Council II. (1964). Lumen Gentium. In The Documents of Vatican II. Vatican: Vatican Publishing House.

90. Vatican Council II. (1964). Lumen Gentium. Retrieved from https://www.vatican.va/archive/hist_councils/ii_vatican_council/documents/vat-ii_const_19641121_lumen-gentium_en.html

91. Vatican Council II. (1965). Nostra Aetate. Retrieved from [URL]

92. Vatican Council II. (1965). Nostra Aetate. Retrieved from http://www.vatican.va/archive/hist_councils/ii_vatican_council/documents/vat-ii_decl_19651028_nostra-aetate_en.html

93. Vatican Council II. (1965). Dei Verbum [Dogmatic Constitution on Divine Revelation].

94. Vatican Council II. (1965a). Gaudium et Spes. Retrieved from https://www.vatican.va/archive/hist_councils/ii_vatican_council/documents/vat-ii_const_19651207_gaudium-et-spes_en.html

95. Vatican Council II. (1965b). Nostra Aetate. Retrieved from https://www.vatican.va/archive/hist_councils/ii_vatican_council/documents/vat-ii_decl_19651028_nostra-aetate_en.html

96. Vatican II. (1965). *Nostra Aetate* (Declaration on the Relation of the Church to Non-Christian Religions).

97. Vatican II. (1965). Nostra Aetate: Declaration on the Relation of the Church to Non-Christian Religions.

98. Ware, K. (1995). The Orthodox Church. Penguin Books.

99. Ware, T. (1993). The Orthodox Church. Penguin Books.

100. Weigel, G. (1992). *A New Worldly Order: John Paul II and Human Freedom*. Eerdmans Publishing Company.

101. Wilken, R. L. (2012). The First Thousand Years: A Global History of Christianity. Yale University Press.

102. Wilkins, W., & Goa, D. (2001). Hinduism: Ancient Traditions and Contemporary Practices. New York: University Press.

103. Xiaogan, L. (2009). The Four Noble Truths: A Study in Historical Context. Journal of Buddhist Studies, 27(1), 12-34.

THE 15 PRAYERS OF ST. BRIDGET

These Prayers and these Promises have been copied from a book printed in Toulouse in 1740 and published by the P. Adrien Parvilliers of the Company of Jesus, Apostolic Missionary of the Holy Land, with approbation, permission and recommendation to distribute them.

Pope Pius IX took cognisance of these Prayers with the prologue; he approved them May 31, 1862, recognising them as true and for the good of souls.

As St. Bridget for a long time wanted to know the number of blows Our Lord received during His Passion, He one day appeared to her and said: "I received 5480 blows on My Body. If you wish to honour them in some way, say 15 Our Fathers and 15 Hail Marys with the following Prayers (which He taught her) for a whole year. When the year is up, you will have honoured each one of My Wounds."

He made the following promises to anyone who recited these Prayers for a whole year:

1. I will deliver 15 souls of his lineage from Purgatory.

2. 15 souls of his lineage will be confirmed and preserved in grace.

3. 15 sinners of his lineage will be converted.

4. Whoever recites these Prayers will attain the first degree of perfection.

5. 15 days before his death I will give him My Precious Body in order that he may escape eternal starvation; I will give him My Precious Blood to drink lest he thirst eternally.

6. 15 days before his death he will feel a deep contrition for all his sins and will have a perfect knowledge of them.

7. I will place before him the sign of My Victorious Cross for his help and defence against the attacks of his enemies.

8. Before his death I shall come with My Dearest Beloved Mother.

9. I shall graciously receive his soul, and will lead it into eternal joys.

10. And having led it there I shall give him a special draught from the fountain of My Deity, something I will not for those who have not recited My Prayers.

11. Let it be known that whoever may have been living in a state of mortal sin for 30 years, but who will

recite devoutly, or have the intention to recite these Prayers, the Lord will forgive him all his sins.

12. I shall protect him from strong temptations.

13. I shall preserve and guard his 5 senses.

14. I shall preserve him from a sudden death.

15. His soul will be delivered from eternal death.

16. He will obtain all he asks for from God and the Blessed Virgin.

17. If he has lived all his life doing his own will and he is to die the next day, his life will be prolonged.

18. Every time one recites these Prayers he gains 100 days indulgence.

19. He is assured of being joined to the supreme Choir of Angels.

20. Whoever teaches these Prayers to another, will have continuous joy and merit which will endure eternally.

21. There where these Prayers are being said or will be said in the future God is present with His grace.

Each prayer is preceded by one Our Father and one Hail Mary.

Our Father, who art in heaven, hallowed be thy name. Thy kingdom come.

Thy will be done on earth as it is in heaven.

Give us this day our daily bread and forgive us our trespasses as we forgive those who trespass against us and lead us not into temptation but deliver us from evil. **Amen**

Hail Mary, full of grace, the Lord is with thee; blessed art thou among women and blessed is the fruit of thy womb, Jesus.

Holy Mary, Mother of God, pray for us sinners, now and at the hour of our death. **Amen.**

FIRST PRAYER

Our Father – Hail Mary.

O Jesus Christ! Eternal Sweetness to those who love Thee, joy surpassing all joy and all desire, Salvation and Hope of all sinners, Who hast proved that Thou hast no greater desire than to be among men, even assuming human nature at the fullness of time for the love of men, recall all the sufferings Thou hast endured from the instant of Thy conception, and especially during Thy Passion, as it was decreed and ordained from all eternity in the Divine plan.

Remember, O Lord, that during the Last Supper with Thy disciples, having washed their feet, Thou gavest them Thy Most Precious Body and Blood, and while at the same time thou didst sweetly console them, Thou didst foretell them Thy coming Passion.

Remember the sadness and bitterness which Thou didst experience in Thy Soul as Thou Thyself bore witness saying: "My Soul is sorrowful even unto death."

Remember all the fear, anguish and pain that Thou didst suffer in Thy delicate Body before the torment of the Crucifixion, when, after having prayed three times, bathed in a sweat of blood, Thou wast betrayed by Judas, Thy disciple, arrested by the people of a nation Thou hadst chosen and elevated, accused by false witnesses, unjustly judged by three judges during the flower of Thy youth and during the solemn Paschal season.

Remember that Thou wast despoiled of Thy garments and clothed in those of derision; that Thy Face and Eyes were veiled, that Thou wast buffeted, crowned with thorns, a reed placed in Thy Hands, that Thou was crushed with blows and overwhelmed with affronts and outrages.

In memory of all these pains and sufferings which Thou didst endure before Thy Passion on the Cross, grant me before my death true contrition, a sincere and entire confession, worthy satisfaction and the remission of all my sins. **Amen.**

SECOND PRAYER

Our Father – Hail Mary.

O Jesus! True liberty of angels, Paradise of delights, remember the horror and sadness which Thou didst endure when Thy enemies, like furious lions, surrounded Thee, and by thousands of insults, spits, blows, lacerations and other unheard-of-cruelties, tormented Thee at will.

In consideration of these torments and insulting words, I beseech Thee, O my Saviour, to deliver me from all my enemies, visible and invisible, and to bring me, under Thy protection, to the perfection of eternal salvation. **Amen.**

THIRD PRAYER

Our Father – Hail Mary.

O Jesus! Creator of Heaven and earth Whom nothing can encompass or limit, Thou Who dost enfold and hold all under Thy Loving power, remember the very bitter pain.

Thou didst suffer when the Jews nailed Thy Sacred Hands and Feet to the Cross by blow after blow with big blunt nails, and not finding Thee in a pitiable enough state to satisfy their rage, they enlarged Thy Wounds, and added pain to

pain, and with indescribable cruelty stretched Thy Body
on the Cross, pulled Thee from all sides, thus dislocating Thy
Limbs.

I beg of Thee, O Jesus, by the memory of this most Loving
suffering of the Cross, to grant me the grace to fear Thee
and to Love Thee. **Amen.**

FOURTH PRAYER
Our Father – Hail Mary.
O Jesus! Heavenly Physician, raised aloft on the Cross to
heal our wounds with Thine, remember the bruises which
Thou didst suffer and the weakness of all Thy Members
which were distended to such a degree that never was there
pain like unto Thine.

From the crown of Thy Head to the Soles of Thy Feet there
was not one spot on Thy Body that was not in torment, and
yet, forgetting all Thy sufferings, Thou didst not cease to
pray to Thy Heavenly Father for Thy enemies, saying:
"Father forgive them for they know not what they do."

Through this great Mercy, and in memory of this suffering,
grant that the remembrance of Thy Most Bitter Passion may

effect in us a perfect contrition and the remission of all our sins. **Amen**.

FIFTH PRAYER

Our Father – Hail Mary.

O Jesus! Mirror of eternal splendour, remember the sadness which Thou experienced, when contemplating in the light of Thy Divinity the predestination of those who would be saved by the merits of Thy Sacred Passion.

Thou didst see at the same time, the great multitude of reprobates who would be damned for their sins, and Thou didst complain bitterly of those hopeless lost and unfortunate sinners.

Through this abyss of compassion and pity, and especially through the goodness which Thou displayed to the good thief when Thou saidst to him: "This day, thou shalt be with Me in Paradise." I beg of Thee, O Sweet Jesus, that at the hour of my death, Thou wilt show me mercy. **Amen**.

SIXTH PRAYER

Our Father – Hail Mary.

O Jesus! Beloved and most desirable King, remember the grief Thou didst suffer, when naked and like a common criminal.

Thou was fastened and raised on the Cross, when all Thy relatives and friends abandoned Thee, except Thy Beloved Mother, who remained close to Thee during Thy agony and whom Thou didst entrust to Thy faithful disciple when Thou saidst to Mary: "Woman, behold thy son!" and to St. John: "Son, behold thy Mother!"

I beg of Thee O my Saviour, by the sword of sorrow which pierced the soul of Thy holy Mother, to have compassion on me in all my affliction and tribulations, both corporal and spiritual, and to assist me in all my trials, and especially at the hour of my death. **Amen**.

SEVENTH PRAYER
Our Father - Hail Mary.
O Jesus! Inexhaustible Fountain of compassion, Who by a profound gesture of Love, said from the Cross: "I thirst!" suffered from the thirst for the salvation of the human race.

I beg of Thee O my Saviour, to inflame in our hearts the

desire to tend toward perfection in all our acts; and to extinguish in us the concupiscence of the flesh and the ardor of worldly desires. **Amen.**

EIGHTH PRAYER

Our Father – Hail Mary.

O Jesus! Sweetness of hearts, delight of the spirit, by the bitterness of the vinegar and gall which Thou didst taste on the Cross for Love of us, grant us the grace to receive worthily.

Thy Precious Body and Blood during our life and at the hour of our death, that they may serve as a remedy and consolation for our souls. **Amen.**

NINTH PRAYER

Our Father – Hail Mary.

O Jesus! Royal virtue, joy of the mind, recall the pain Thou didst endure when, plunged in an ocean of bitterness at the approach of death, insulted, outraged by the Jews.

Thou didst cry out in a loud voice that Thou was abandoned by Thy Father, saying: "My God, My God, why hast Thou forsaken me?"

Through this anguish, I beg of Thee, O my Saviour, not to abandon me in the terrors and pains of my death. **Amen.**

TENTH PRAYER

Our Father – Hail Mary.

O Jesus! Who art the beginning and end of all things, life and virtue, remembers that for our sakes Thou was plunged in an abyss of suffering from the soles of Thy Feet to the crown of Thy Head.

In consideration of the enormity of Thy Wounds, teach me to keep, through pure love, Thy Commandments, whose way is wide and easy for those who love Thee. **Amen.**

ELEVENTH PRAYER

Our Father – Hail Mary.

O Jesus! Deep abyss of mercy, I beg of Thee, in memory of Thy Wounds which penetrated to the very marrow of Thy Bones and to the depth of Thy being, to draw me, a miserable sinner, overwhelmed by my offenses, away from sin and to hide me from Thy Face justly irritated against me, hide me in Thy wounds, until Thy anger and just indignation shall have passed away. **Amen.**

TWELFTH PRAYER

Our Father – Hail Mary.

O Jesus! Mirror of Truth, symbol of unity, bond of charity, remember the multitude of wounds with which Thou wast afflicted from head to foot, torn and reddened by the spilling of Thy adorable Blood. O great and universal pain, which Thou didst suffer in Thy virginal flesh for love of us! Sweetest Jesus! What is there that Thou couldst have done for us which Thou has not done!

May the fruit of Thy suffering be renewed in my soul by the faithful remembrance of Thy Passion, and may Thy love increase in my heart each day, until I see Thee in eternity: Thou Who art the treasure of every real good and every joy, which I beg Thee to grant me, O Sweetest Jesus, in heaven. **Amen.**

THIRTEENTH PRAYER

Our Father – Hail Mary.

O Jesus! Strong Lion, Immortal and Invincible King,

remember the pain which Thou didst endure when all Thy
strength, both moral and physical, was entirely exhausted,
Thou didst bow Thy Head, saying: "It is consummated!"

Through this anguish and grief, I beg of Thee Lord Jesus, to
have mercy on me at the hour of my death when my mind
will be greatly troubled and my soul will be in
anguish. **Amen.**

FOURTEENTH PRAYER
Our Father – Hail Mary.
O Jesus! Only Son of the Father, Splendour and Figure of His
Substance, remember the simple and humble
recommendation.

Thou didst make of Thy Soul to Thy Eternal Father, saying:
"Father, into Thy Hands I commend My Spirit!" And with Thy
Body all torn, and Thy Heart Broken, and the bowels of
Thy Mercy open to redeem us, Thou didst Expire.

By this Precious Death, I beg of Thee O King of Saints,
comfort me and help me to resist the devil, the flesh and the
world, so that being dead to the world I may live for Thee
alone.

I beg of Thee at the hour of my death to receive me, a pilgrim and an exile returning to Thee. **Amen.**

FIFTEENTH PRAYER

Our Father – Hail Mary.

O Jesus! True and fruitful Vine! Remember the abundant outpouring of Blood which Thou didst so generously shed from Thy Sacred Body as juice from grapes in a wine press.

From Thy Side, pierced with a lance by a soldier, blood and water issued forth until there was not left in Thy Body a single drop, and finally, like a bundle of myrrh lifted to the top of the Cross Thy delicate Flesh was destroyed, the very Substance of Thy Body withered, and the Marrow of Thy Bones dried up.

Through this bitter Passion and through the outpouring of Thy Precious Blood, I beg of Thee, O Sweet Jesus, to receive my soul when I am in my death agony. **Amen.**

CONCLUSION

O Sweet Jesus! Pierce my heart so that my tears of

penitence and love will be my bread day and night; may I be converted entirely to Thee, may my heart be Thy perpetual habitation, may my conversation be pleasing to Thee, and may the end of my life be so praiseworthy that I may merit Heaven and there with Thy saints, praise Thee

forever. **Amen.**

9 798330 276097